Channel Markers

Channel Markers

Wisdom from the Ten Commandments and the Sermon on the Mount

William G. Enright

Geneva Press
Louisville, Kentucky

Scripture quotations from the New Revised Standard
Version of the Bible are copyright © 1989 by the Division
of Christian Education of the National Council of the Churches
of Christ in the U.S.A. and are used by permission.

Book design by Sharon Adams
Cover design by Lisa Buckley
Photo on cover by Capt. David R. Appleton

First edition
Published by Geneva Press
Louisville, Kentucky

PRINTED IN THE UNITED STATES OF AMERICA

01 02 03 04 05 06 07 08 09 10 — 10 9 8 7 6 5 4 3 2

Library of Congress Cataloging-in-Publication Data

Enright, William G.
    Channel markers: wisdom from the Ten Commandments and the
    Sermon on the Mount / William G. Enright. — 1st ed.
    p. cm.
    Includes bibliographical references.
    ISBN 0-664-50182-6 (alk. paper)
    1. Ten commandments. 2. Beatitudes. I. Title.

BV4655.E57 2001
    241.5—dc21   2001033340

To Second Presbyterian Church,
Indianapolis, Indiana,
my family of faith.

Contents

Acknowledgments   ix

I. The Ten Commandments

1. Priorities:
   The First and Second Commandments   3
2. Integrity:
   The Third Commandment   11
3. Time:
   The Fourth Commandment   19
4. Memory:
   The Fifth Commandment   27
5. Reverence:
   The Sixth and Seventh Commandments   35
6. Manners:
   The Eighth, Ninth, and Tenth Commandments   43

II. The Sermon on the Mount

7. Heading for the Open Sea   53
8. Living as If   61
9. Living as if the World Were a Safe Place   69
10. Living as if You Were a Really Good Person   77
11. Living as if God Were Your Only Audience   85

Notes   93

Acknowledgments

*F*aith comes to life in community and family; as Saint Paul observed: "Together, we are the body of Christ." I am blessed to be part of a very special family of faith, the Second Presbyterian Church of Indianapolis, Indiana. It was to this family that these thoughts were first expressed in the form of sermons. It was a friend and member of this worshiping family, Craig Dykstra, who suggested that these sermons be put into manuscript form. It was the Session (the governing board) of this family, together with Dr. Joan Malick, my very special colleague who serves as our executive minister/head of staff, and Lyn Milan, my faithful executive secretary of twenty years, who freed me from my administrative responsibilities to focus on the proclamation of the Word. In the larger family of faith, it has been my editor, Tom Long, who, with the savvy unique to a preacher and teacher of preachers par excellence, has nuanced a collection of sermons into a book of readings. Finally, project editor Ella Brazley has shepherded this manuscript through its final production with wise and gracious counsel. To all of these people and many more, I am grateful.

Above all, I am indebted to my blood family as they continually help me to grow in the meaning of faith and love. My mother, Lucille, now ninety-five, made certain that the story was told and passed along to me in both word and deed. My two sons, Scott and Kirk, and their families bless me by

loving me enough to keep me honest and open to the wisdom
and questions of succeeding generations. "Grampa Bill," my
grandchildren will say as I read or tell them a story, "how can
that be?" or "why did God say that?" Most of all, it is my wife
Edie, the greatest gift I have been given, who as my lover and
cheerleader graces me with God's presence as my best and
cherished friend.

Epiphany 2001

PART 1 The Ten Commandments

Chapter 1

Priorities: The First
and Second Commandments

You shall have no other gods before me. . . . You shall
not make for yourself an idol, . . . for I the LORD
your God am a jealous God.

—Ex. 20:3–5

 recent issue of the *New Yorker* carried a "Millennium Travel Advisory." It began with the
question: "Where will you be on the ultimate
New Year's Eve?" It then touted the options
available around the world for the big bash at the turn of the
new century, from Nantucket to Nepal to Fiji. Where were
you on New Year's Eve 2000? I was at home, and, from what
I read, most of you were at home as well. We stayed home
with all that canned food and bottled water we purchased just
in case. We stayed home because the turning of the odome-
ter on civilization left us just a tad queasy.

This leap into a new millennium is something no living
human has ever experienced before. Think about it: The last
time we humans lived through such a momentous turning of the
calendar, the Song dynasty governed China, the Byzantine
Empire stretched across Turkey and parts of Greece, German
kings ruled the Holy Roman Empire, feudalism reigned in most
of Europe and Great Britain, the Toltec Empire was emerging
in Mexico, and the United States of America was yet to be

discovered by Europeans. Most people were poor and illiterate, infant mortality was normative, life expectancy was short.[1]

How will citizens of this universe see us at the next turning of the millennial calendar? A *New York Times* writer responded to that question:

> They . . .will wonder about us. They'll call us the Greeks of our time, widely known, accomplished, broadly influential, even respected, but . . . baffling. . . . As one of our 20th century poets has put it: "Men die miserably every day/for lack/of what is found there."[2]

My mother celebrated her ninety-fourth birthday between Christmas and New Year's. I asked her, "Mom, did you ever think you would live into a new millennium?" Of course not, she said. I confess that this momentous turning of the calendar also put me in touch with my own finitude and left me asking myself an old question: How, now, should I live?

A year or so ago, billboards bearing teasing messages from God began to appear on roads all across America. The signs read:

> *Do you have any idea where you're going?*
>
> God
>
> *Need directions?*
>
> God
>
> *I can think of ten things that are carved in stone.*
>
> God

I invite you to muse with me about those ten things carved in stone. Ironically, we don't all agree on how we should read the Ten Commandments. Like that Alabama judge who, last year, made a fuss about posting the Ten Commandments in his courtroom, you can read them as cold, legalistic absolutes drawn like lines in the sand that, once crossed, mean judgment. Like Ted Koppel, in a commencement address delivered at Duke University, you can read them as ethical guidelines intended to resolve all moral problems. They do have something to say about morals and ethics, but they hardly resolve all moral dilemmas. For example, we don't agree when it comes to "You shall not kill," so we argue over war and capital punishment and abortion. I think there is another way to read these Ten Commandments: It is to see them as channel markers given to guide us in our quest for the good and holy life.

Channel markers remind me that I am on a journey. Sometimes I feel like a giant cruise ship sailing across a big ocean. I am free to choose my course as I zig and zag here and there. Yet, if I am going to make a safe passage, I need also to know where the shoals and rocks and barrier reefs are located. At other times, I feel like a fragile sailboat negotiating a treacherous waterway laced with rapids and waterfalls and dangerous currents. It is the channel markers that invite me to live carefully, for life is a journey with choices to be made and values to be pursued and priorities to be set. We humans are not God's puppets; we are God's children blessed with lives to be lived.

In the Bible, the Ten Commandments are found in two places: Exodus 20 and Deuteronomy 5. In Exodus, the Hebrew people are but three months out of Egypt. Moses is setting up his regime. As a fledgling nation still sorting out what it means to be God's people, they need channel markers to guide them in their journey. By the time the book of Deuteronomy is completed, hundreds of years have passed The Hebrews have journeyed through the wilderness and occupied the Promised Land. They have become a nation. Many kings, including David and Solomon, have come and gone. They have fought wars; some they have won and others they have lost. Now they are being held hostage in Babylonia.

They need channel markers to set the perimeters for their living in an alien land.

Our first two channel markers read, "You shall have no other gods before me" and "You shall not make for yourself an idol." What do these sayings mean? As a recent catechism reads, they mean, "No loyalty comes before my loyalty to God."[3] In other words, this initial channel marker, set forth by the first two commandments, simply says, "Put God first!" Alexander Solzhenitsyn, looking back over everything that happened in Russia in the twentieth century, said that it happened because "People have forgotten God!"

Priorities! Put God first! Why? Because only then will you know who and whose you are. God commands and we respond because we were made to live in relationship with God. God made us to be his children. Check out all ten of those things carved in stone. They tell us that the good and holy life depends upon how we choose to relate to God and to each other.

In the novel *The Solitaire Mystery*, author Jostein Gaarder chronicles the conversation between a twelve-year-old boy named Hans and his father as they travel by car through Europe. They are on their way to Athens when Hans asks the question, "Dad, do you believe in God? If God really exists, then he's clever at playing hide-and-seek with His creations." Laughing, his dad replies, "Maybe He was frightened when He saw what He'd created. . . . But mind you, I agree He could at least have signed the masterpiece before He took off." "Signed it?" asks a puzzled Hans. His father explains, "He could easily have carved His name into a canyon or something . . . [but] He didn't leave his calling card behind."[4]

Reflecting upon the meaning of these first two commandments, John Calvin says that God did leave behind a signature and a calling card. God did not want his image reduced to brick or stone or mortar or granite because God had already put his image in skin and bone, in you and me. These first channel markers tell us that God puts a big price tag on our relationship with him. They remind us who and whose we are! We are individuals created in God's image, every one of us.[5]

Priorities! Put God first! Why? Because God is dangerous—so dangerous that God must always be handled with care. Read the fine print at the bottom of these first channel markers: "I the LORD your God am a jealous God." God is a lover who will not tolerate other suitors. This jealous God will not settle for our mere belief in his existence. He wants all of us: our hearts, our minds, our time, our genitals, our pots and pans, our jobs and our careers, all our social relationships. As the Old Testament scholar Walter Brueggemann observes, the God of the Bible is "irascible and hot-tempered, odd and unpredictable, . . . wondrous and awesome."[6] Ignore God and God goes away leaving us grounded on the shoals of our own choosing.

Priorities! Put God first! Why? Because this dangerous God is counting on us; we are all God has in this world. Two Duke University professors, Stanley Hauerwas and William Willimon, put it well: "The commandments signal to us that this thing between us and God matters. God desires us and enlists our aid in reclaiming a lost creation. The salvation of the world turns on our obedience, on how we have sex, and handle property and watch our words."[7]

Priorities! Put God first! Why? Because you and I need God if we are going to live well and whole. Listen to the rest of the fine print found at the bottom of these initial channel markers: "I the LORD your God am a jealous God . . . but [I show] steadfast love to the thousandth generation of those who love me."

When Moses comes down the mountain, proudly carrying in his arms the two stone tablets engraved with the Ten Commandments, he discovers the implausible. While Moses was on the mountain with God, his brother, Aaron, has collected all the gold the people brought with them in their escape from Egypt, melted it down, and created an idol, a golden calf. As Moses stands back and watches, the people, in a frenzy of revelry, dance and party around the golden calf, worshiping the idol as if it were a god. Beside himself and in a fit of rage, Moses takes the tablets on which God has etched the commandments and slams them to the ground, shattering them into a thousand pieces.

Next comes the surprise. This jealous, odd, unpredictable, wonderful, awesome, irascible God summons Moses back up the mountain, where he gifts him with a new set of stone tablets. Moses and the Hebrew people can begin again. God is a God of steadfast love. That means shocking mercy and unexpected new beginnings.

I need God because I need mercy and love from beyond myself if I am to live well. I have a knack for ignoring the channel markers and ending up crashed on the barrier reefs of my making. The sixteenth-century English poet John Donne wrote for us all:

> Wilt Thou forgive that sin where I begun,
>   Which is my sin, though it were done before?
> Wilt Thou forgive that sin through which I run,
>   And do run still, though still I do deplore?
>   When Thou hast done, Thou hast not done,
>   For I have more.
>
> Wilt Thou forgive that sin by which I have won
>   Others to sin? and made my sin their door?
> Wilt Thou forgive that sin which I did shun
>   A year or two, but wallowed in a score?
>   When Thou hast done, Thou hast not done,
>   For I have more.[8]

We all "have more," don't we? Our problem is that we cannot erase the past on our own. We cannot undo what has been done. We are stuck with our yesterdays. Only God can forgive.

Recently we said farewell to Charles Schultz, creator of the comic strip *Peanuts*. Some of you may recall one *Peanuts* strip where Linus, feeling anxious, says, "I guess it's wrong, always to be worrying about tomorrow. Maybe we should think only about today." Charlie Brown replies, "No, that's giving up. I'm still hoping that yesterday will get better." I need this channel marker called "Priorities! Put God first!" because only God can forgive and only forgiveness can make yesterday better!

The odd thing about these Ten Commandments is they are conditional; you can take them seriously or you can choose to ignore them. The first words out of God's mouth to Moses that day at Sinai were not "You shall have no other gods before me, etc. etc., etc.," but "Now therefore, if you obey my voice" (Ex. 19:5). The Ten Commandments are not for humanity in general; they are only for those who want to partner with God and live to make a difference in this new millennium.

Chapter 2

Integrity:
The Third Commandment

You shall not make wrongful use
of the name of the LORD your God.

—Ex. 20:7

spotted a bumper sticker years ago: "God's last name isn't damn!" Instantly, the Third Commandment came to mind: "You shall not make wrongful use of the name of the LORD your God."

My hunch is that when most of us think of the Third Commandment, we think of it as a prohibition against swearing. In reality, this commandment has very little to do with profanity; its focus is on something much more weighty than swearing.

My first church was on the south side of Chicago. Chicago developed as a collection of ethnic neighborhoods: Norwegians around Logan Square, Poles in Cicero, Jews on Maxwell Street, the Dutch in Roseland. Roseland was where my church was located. Within a one-mile radius of that church there were a dozen Reformed or Christian Reformed congregations. The Dutch people, I discovered, take the Ten Commandments seriously.

A Dutch realtor told me this story. He was building a Tinker Toy windmill with his young son. They were having trouble getting the windmill to stand upright. Finally, in a fit of frustration, his son took his fist and smashed the Tinker Toys to the floor as he shouted, "Damn it!" Taken aback, his father said, "Tommy, we don't use that kind of language in this house. Our family doesn't talk that way." Tommy grew silent, staring at the floor. Finally, turning to his father, he asked with the kind of innocence only a child can muster, "Daddy, would it make it all right if I said, 'God damn it'?"

That is what the Third Commandment is all about. It speaks to our tendency to try to use God to make everything we do or are about all right. From athletics, to politics, to business, to everyday life, we use God-talk to win games and elections, to one-up or put down other people, to manipulate deals, and to baptize our personal causes with God's name in an attempt to make ourselves look good. This Third Commandment is probably the most violated of all the commandments, and it is religious people who most frequently abuse it. A fine new catechism produced by the Presbyterian Church (U.S.A.) reads:

> Question: What do you learn from the third commandment?
> Answer: I should use God's name with reverence and awe. God's name is taken in vain when used to support wrong. It is insulted when used carelessly, as in a curse or pious cliché.[1]

In Exodus 3, Moses finds himself eyeball to eyeball with God. Moses is a fugitive sorting out his future in a strange new land. He has fallen in love and married and is now trying to make points with his father-in-law by taking care of Jethro's goats and sheep. One day as he is out caring for the sheep, God stops Moses dead in his tracks. God speaks, and Moses listens. God drafts Moses for a special assignment, but he is dubious. How is he to explain his mission to the Hebrew people in Egypt? "What shall I say to the people when they ask, 'Who sent you?'" he wants to know. The voice replies, "Say that I am who I am, that I am has sent you to them."

So it was that the ancient Jews took a form of the verb *to be* ("I am") and created the name *YAHWEH*. It was, however, a name they never spoke. For the ancient Jew, *YAHWEH* was a name too sacred to speak. Whenever they came to the word *YAHWEH*, they would simply substitute *Lord* or *My Lord*. God's name was too holy, too special, too revered, too sacred to be reduced to something commonplace.

"You shall not make wrongful use of the name of the LORD your God." Remember, these commandments are not so much legal absolutes and moral imperatives as they are channel markers. Channel markers exist to guide us safely down the waterways of life. They set the perimeters of living while leaving us room to navigate on our own. We are the ones who choose how we will live with these channel markers from God.

The first two commandments, "You shall have no other gods before me" and "You shall not make for yourself an idol," gave birth to our first channel marker: Remember God! Put God first! The second channel marker, based upon the Third Commandment, is equally terse: Integrity! Speak God's name with integrity! This channel marker is aimed to keep us out of the rapids into which we fall when we flaunt God, as well as the shoals on which we become grounded when we take God for granted.

Integrity! Speak God's Name with Integrity. Don't misuse the name of the Lord your God! Don't flaunt God! But we do flaunt God. We religious people are particularly adept at flaunting God. I sat in on a church meeting this week in which this second channel marker was curtly ignored. With the kind of presumptuous piousness only we religious folk can muster, I listened as two people from outside my congregation politicked, then tried to baptize their politicking by telling us that if we followed their way we would experience the "presence of the Holy Spirit and know God's will." I cringed. Does any human have the audacity to speak for God and outline with certainty how God will work? Whenever we presume God, we break the Third Commandment.

In almost every political campaign, I see this second channel marker abused. In the 2000 campaign, the Republican contenders for president met in a round table discussion in Iowa. George W. Bush was asked to identify his favorite philosopher. He replied, "Jesus Christ." Quickly, Gary Bauer, Orrin Hatch, Alan Keyes, and Steve Forbes jumped in and played their religious cards. Not to be outdone by the Republicans, the Democratic candidate, Al Gore, in a December *60 Minutes* segment, described himself as a "born-again Christian." Once again I cringed.

My friends, we must be careful how we play the Jesus card. Do we play it to gain votes and win favors and influence people? Leon Wieseltier, editor of the *New Republic,* says, "Most people in politics don't believe in God; they believe in religion. The genuinely pious people I have known have been very quiet about it."[2] Karl Barth, that great twentieth-century theologian who honed his religious convictions amidst the horrors of Hitler's Germany, counseled that, when it came to politics, "Christians can bring in their Christianity only anonymously."[3] "You shall not make wrongful use of the name of the LORD your God." Don't flaunt God!

I also cringe nearly every time I go to a professional football game. I have no problems with Christian athletes from both teams meeting in the center of the field following the game to join hands and offer a prayer of gratitude to God for those who escaped injury during the game and a prayer for healing grace for those injured in the game. I have, however, serious problems with those athletes who make an end zone show for God every time they score a touchdown, as if to suggest that God enabled them to score the touchdowns.

Does God score touchdowns? When it comes to basketball, does God sink three-point shots at the buzzer to win games or send them into overtime? As I write, it is basketball season in Indiana and we may be in trouble. This past Tuesday night, God clearly favored Michigan State over Indiana when Morris Peterson sank a three-point shot to tie the game and send it into overtime while A. J. Guyton missed a three-point shot which would have won the game for Indiana. The good news is, God apparently prefers Indiana to Illinois. So in Wednesday night's Purdue versus Illinois basketball game, Illinois's Cory Bradford missed a winning three-point shot with just a few seconds to go, while Carson Cunningham sank the winning free throws for Purdue. Now, does anyone really believe that God plays favorites on the basketball court or football field?

Cosmic name-dropping can be misleading, even dangerous. Beware, this second channel marker says, of flaunting God by linking God to your cause or situation. God, whose name is holy, is bigger than you think!

Integrity! Speak God's Name with Integrity! Don't take God for granted! Tragically, many of us do take God for granted. We say our prayers by rote. We join churches merely to fill out our resumes and, in the end, to look good in our obituaries. We inscribe the phrase "In God we trust" on all the money we mint and print without ever pausing to reflect on what that really means. Preachers stand in pulpits mouthing eternal hair-raising truths as if they were nothing more than maudlin platitudes. Meantime, people sit in their pews yawning their way through liturgics they have come to take for granted. The physician and poet William Carlos Williams observed, "People go to church, but the God they worship (if they do that while they're sitting in those pews) isn't 'The Big Man' in their lives after they leave and go home."[4] Duplicity weaves its way through the fabric of our lives when we take God for granted!

In his recent book, *The Secular Mind,* the Harvard psychiatrist Robert Coles tells of a conversation he had years ago with a candid Christian social reformer named Dorothy Day, who told him,

> I love sitting in church praying. . . . I try to be myself and talk to God as honestly and spontaneously as I can. I'm really afraid that going to church and praying will become an automatic thing with me. I'm afraid I'll be going through the motions—that I won't be thinking, or be *myself* praying—that I'll be half conscious, daydreaming. I'm in church seeking the sacred, but I go there as a secular person. . . . You know, when people ask me why I converted, *that's* what I tell them, that I was looking for something beyond this secular life that I've lived to the full. . . . I found that something in a sacred tradition, and so, when I go to church, I try to *live* my religion, *live* that sacred time in that sacred place. . . . I get frightened I'll pick up my old secular ways in church and, while praying, just go through the motions.[5]

"You shall not make wrongful use of the name of the LORD your God." Integrity! Speak God's Name with Integrity! That is why Abraham Lincoln is one of my heroes. He knew how to talk about God without ever presuming to speak for God.

In the summer of 1862, a group of Quakers visited Lincoln to urge him, in God's name, to emancipate the slaves. Sympathetic to their cause, Lincoln announced his willingness to "be an instrument in God's hands" but warned them that "God's way of accomplishing the end of slavery may be different from theirs." Six months later, when Lincoln issued the Emancipation Proclamation, he expressed his own uncertainty over the propriety of his action, saying, "I can only trust in God I have made no mistake. . . .It is now for the country and the world to judge."[6] People who live with integrity live honest to God. They live by God's grace without presuming to speak for God.

In a recent interview, the British novelist Barbara Howatch, a Christian, was asked if it was her intention to evangelize through her novels. She replied, "No, that would be phony. A novelist's first duty is to write a story. A novelist's second duty is to write a readable story. . . . Get the story right and the Christian themes will emerge from the interaction of the characters in the story." Then she made this confession. Before "my religious conversion I worked furthering my own self-interest. . . . Now I offer my books to God to use as he pleases. That sets me free."[7]

"You shall not make wrongful use of the name of the LORD your God." Live your faith with integrity and you will find yourself free to negotiate the waterways of our world without self-destructing on the rapids of flaunting God or becoming grounded on the shoals of taking God for granted. My hunch is that this is the honest-to-God faith for which the world yearns. But take care: These channel markers are not for everyone. They are only for those who want to partner with God and live to make a difference in this new millennium!

Chapter 3

Time:
The Fourth Commandment

Remember the sabbath day, and keep it holy.

—Ex. 20:8

*O*f all the commandments, it is this Fourth Commandment with which I struggle most. Last year was a year of strange grace for me. As usual, I overprogrammed my days, only this time my behavior caught up with me, leaving me with bones that were weary and a soul that was as parched and prickly as a desert cactus in the middle of a summer's sizzle. I had no place in my life for Sabbath.

Of course, I had no one to blame but myself. All my life I prided myself on being in control, which meant planning and staying ahead and, when necessary, micromanaging details to get things done right. For years, I boasted that, except for the summer months, I never took a regular day off. I gloated that my work was my play. Somewhere along the way, I even began to count the hours I worked each week as I headed for church on a Monday morning. Seventy-five hours was a light week, with eighty and ninety hours more commonplace. The odd thing was that, nearly every day, guilt whiplashed my soul because I did not have enough time to attend to something or someone as I should. Missing in my life was what our Jewish friends call *Shabbat,* what we know of as *Sabbath.*

My hunch is that many of you resonate with what I am saying. Ironically, some of you were my models and heroes in this mad dash to live in control. Between 1968 and 1988, the average worker has added in excess of 160 hours to his or her work year, which calculates to be an extra month of work. I wanted to keep up. I wanted you to know that ministers really do work more than one day a week!

One day last winter I looked into the mirror. What I saw got my attention: My stomach and my jowls were sagging, along with my soul. In my busyness in doing "God's work," I had left no place for God in *my* everyday world. That cistern deep within me called my soul was empty. One night, after we had once again given up our symphony tickets so I could work on a sermon, I looked at my wife and I said, "Edie, if this is living, I've had it. I can't keep this up. It's not fair to you, to me, to God. Either I change or this will be my last year as the pastor of Second Presbyterian Church."

There are two versions of this Fourth Commandment. The wording is identical, but the rationales are different. In Deuteronomy 5:15, the reason for this commandment is that the Hebrews in Egypt went four hundred years without a day off. The upshot was they were no longer persons; they were slaves. They were like pieces of machinery neatly packaged in skin and bone. They existed merely to make bricks and build pyramids. Don't miss the point: Make no place for Sabbath in your life and in time you will become a slave, a person whose humanity has been defaced.

In Exodus 20:8, the second place where we find these Ten Commandments, we are encouraged to keep the Sabbath because God kept it. Think about that! God did his work in six days, after which God paused to catch his breath! One day a week even God sat down just to be. Sabbath, as writer Eugene Peterson reminds us, means quit! Let go! Take a break! "The word itself has nothing devout or holy in it. It is a word about time . . . about what we usually call wasting time."[1] Sabbath has to do with finding a quiet center out of which to survive the busyness of life.

Remember, these Ten Commandments are not legal absolutes and rigid moral imperatives; they are channel markers. Channel markers set the boundaries to guide us as we negotiate our way down the waterways of our busy worlds. The channel marker reflecting the Fourth Commandment consists of one word: Time!

Time! Time matters! Think about how we talk about time. We say things like "Time flies" or "Time talks." Because time is precious, we put people down who "kill time" or "waste time." The poet William Carlos Williams called time "a storm in which we are all lost."[2] Lawyers bill by the minute, counselors by the hour, consultants by the day. Time is both our god and our enemy.

The truth lurking behind this commandment is this: Time need not be our enemy. Time is God's gift to us. Time is meant to be "a meeting place, a point of rendezvous with God."[3] "Remember the sabbath day, and keep it holy." Something becomes *holy* when we set it aside for God. It is in *time* that we meet God.

The theologian Karl Barth called this Fourth Commandment "the commandment that explains all the other commandments."[4] If we don't make a place for the worship of God at the center of our lives, the first three commandments, which pertain to how we relate to God, become irrelevant, and the last six commandments, which have to do with how we relate to each other, become inconsequential.

Time! How do we make time our friend rather than our enemy? This commandment gives us two clues: rhythm and ritual.

There is a rhythm to life. You and I experience it every day: sunrise and sunset, high tide and low tide, morning and evening. Disrupt the rhythm and chaos sets in. Genesis and Exodus inform us that there is also a rhythm to how we were created to live: Six days we work; one day we rest. Six days we work; one day we rest.

The rhythm of creation is like the rhythm of music. As a boy taking piano lessons, I was told that if I were going to learn to play the piano I had to learn to count to catch the rhythm. Perhaps you remember the drill: one-a-and, two-a-and, one-a-and, two-a-and; one-and, two-and, three-and, one-and, two-and, three-and, and so forth. Six days we work; one day we rest; six days we work, one day we rest. Ignore the rhythm of music and the sound becomes discordant. Disrupt the rhythm of life as God intends it and dissonance sets in; we become slaves rather than human beings.

Ritual is how we keep God's rhythm in our lives. Rituals are prescribed ways of doing things. Rituals keep us honest about who we really are. Rituals are those quiet but powerful experiences that regenerate us and free us to live. Rituals put us in touch with the rhythms of eternity.

Biblical scholars say that it was this ritual of keeping the Sabbath that enabled the Hebrew people to keep their identity when they lived as hostages in alien Babylonia. It was Sabbath worship practiced under the cover of darkness that enabled the early Christians to survive and live life with an uncommon purpose when the Roman Empire was hounding them to death.

Sabbath is a ritual that dares us to come apart and quiet down as we call "time out" to the pressures of a busy schedule and imagine life, not as it is at two hundred miles per hour but as God sees it to be—moving at less than a snail's pace. Remember how the psalmist phrased it: "A thousand years in your sight are like yesterday" (Ps. 90:4). Rituals do more than mirror society's values; they alter and disrupt them. Rituals invite us to live in another world as they dare us to see reality as it really is!

Dorothy Bass, in a superb new book on time, shares this personal story. At age thirty, she was abandoned by the one she loved and left to brood in pain and loneliness. Attempting to begin a new chapter, she moved to Providence, Rhode Island, to continue her graduate studies. Church, with its rich rituals of the Christian year, had always been part of her life. Stuck in darkness, however, she decided to leave the church altogether—not just a particular church, but *the* church, all of it. Christmas came and went—no church. New Year's arrived, and she left a party early, "feeling emptier than ever." It was a long winter. She continues:

> Then came Maundy Thursday, and I could not resist the pull of the story. Around the corner from my apartment was a large church that offered a service in its stately sanctuary. I slipped into a back pew and listened, grateful to be able to blend in with the crowd, anonymous.
>
> On Friday, I went to another church to pray at noon. By Sunday, I wanted to hear the next part of the story so badly that I went again. What I heard caught me off guard, so vivid did it seem, and so directly addressed to me. On the first day of the week, women go to the tomb with spices to honor the dead body of their teacher. . . . But the body is gone. . . . Christ had risen. No, Christ is risen. Hearing this story as if for the first time, . . . I was drawn into a story in which life prevails over death. . . . It graced me with the assurance that I am known, not from outside time but from within it. . . . I was blessed . . . at thirty-one to see the Risen Christ with the eyes of my heart.[5]

It was not busyness that broke the rhythm of life for Dorothy Bass, it was woundedness. It was ritual that brought her back both her rhythm and her life.

There is an old Jewish legend that talks about God's giving the law to Israel. God said, "My children! If you accept the Law and observe my commandments, I will give you for all eternity a thing most precious that I have in my possession." "And what is that precious thing?" the people of Israel asked. "The world to come!" God replied. "Show us an example of the world to come," they responded. God answered, "The Sabbath is an example of the world to come."[6]

Time! Taking time for God! Taking time for yourself! Sabbath has as much to do with playing as it has to do with praying. Remember those two versions of this commandment? Exodus talks about praying and making a place for God. Deuteronomy talks about playing and wasting time for God's glory and our good. To take this Fourth Commandment seriously is to make a place for both play and prayer in your cycle of days.

During Shabbat in observant Jewish homes, families eat together, walk, read together, people dress up and celebrate a special meal together. Married couples enjoy sexual intercourse together. Parents bless their children.[7] On Sunday morning, John Calvin led his congregation in prayers. On Sunday afternoon, John Calvin played skittles (bowled) with the people of Geneva.[8]

Rhythm and ritual! Praying and playing! Six days we work; one day we rest and catch our breath. Last spring, I was ready to say this was my last year. Now I'm ready to stay. Why? Because I'm listening to the rhythm of creation and I'm working on rituals. Water is beginning to seep back into this cistern I call my soul.

At home, my study is upstairs. This year I am trying to begin each day with God—not just waving my schedule in the air and saying, "Run with me, Jesus," as I used to do as I headed out the door, but sitting down and reflecting, meditating, praying. As I climb the stairs in the morning, I say to myself, "I'm going to meet God." About half of the time, I don't make it up those stairs. I have a breakfast meeting or I've done it again and packed my schedule too full. Practice does not make perfect, but it does make life better. As I am rediscovering the rhythm of creation, I'm finding myself more alert to life and more attentive to time and to what God may be about in my time.

Moses is standing on Mount Pisgah. The mountain stands at the edge of the wilderness, so Moses can look into the Promised Land. For forty years, Moses has been leading his people to this moment of claiming the Promised Land. The tragedy is this: Moses is dying; he will never set foot in the Promised Land and he knows it. Moses has run out of time.

As an old tradition has it, Moses speaks the words of Psalm 90 as he stands looking at what will be after he is dead. The psalm talks about the two time zones in which we live. There is the time zone that preoccupies our lives: minutes, hours, days, weeks, years. Then there is God's time zone called eternity, which stretches "from everlasting to everlasting." The psalmist uses words such as *dust* and *dream* and *grass* and *toil* and *trouble* to describe life in our time zone. Yet, the tenor of the psalm is not cosmic homelessness but cosmic hopefulness. Why? Because the time zone in which we play out our lives is a stage that runs from everlasting to everlasting. Because eternity sits in our bones, we can take time seriously.

> Lord, you have been our dwelling place
>   in all generations.
> Before the mountains were brought forth,
>   or ever you had formed the earth and the world,
>   from everlasting to everlasting you are God.
>   . . . .
> For a thousand years in your sight
>   are like yesterday when it is past,
>   or like a watch in the night.
> You sweep them away; they are like a dream,
>   like grass that is renewed in the morning;
> in the morning it flourishes and is renewed;
>   in the evening it fades and withers.
>   . . . .
> The days of our life are seventy years,
>   or perhaps eighty, if we are strong;

even then their span is only toil and trouble;
    they are soon gone, and we fly away.

. . . .

So teach us to count our days
    that we may gain a wise heart.

In the end, if God's time clock is all that matters, then we can embrace time here and now as our friend. God holds us in his eternal care and keeping, from everlasting to everlasting, which leaves us free to count our days as gifts from God—one day at a time.

Six days we work; one day we rest. Six days we work; one day we rest. Rhythm and ritual. Praying and playing. Time! Time to live life whole, but only if we take time for both God and ourselves.

But remember, these channel markers are only for those who want to partner their lives with God and live life with a difference in this new millennium.

Chapter 4

Memory:
The Fifth Commandment

Honor your father and your mother,
so that your days may be long in the land.

—Ex. 20:12

A quotation in a journal article caught my eye:
"Memory is what makes our lives. Life without memory is no life at all." In a book of clinical tales, the psychiatrist Oliver Sacks tells the story of a man named Jimmie G., who was suffering from a neurological loss. Jimmie's memory stopped at the end of World War II. Jimmie was in his fifties, but he saw himself to be nineteen. He could speak, but he could not remember people or incidents five minutes later. One day, following a visit with Jimmie, Dr. Sacks made this notation: "He is, as it were, isolated in a single moment of being, with a moat of forgetting all around him. He is a man without a past (or future) stuck in a constantly changing, meaningless moment."[1]

"Remember!" is the channel marker reflecting the fifth commandment. "Life without memory is no life at all!"

Remember! Remember your parents! This Fifth Commandment is for children, especially for adult children. The focus of this commandment is on aging parents. We may not all be married. We all don't have children. Never, however, do we cease to be children of parents. And we never stop talking about our parents regardless of how old we are or how long our parents may have been dead. As Shirley Abbot describes it, "Our ancestors live in "our mind's attic."[2]

"Honor your father and your mother." There is more to *honor* than remembering. *Honor* has to do with prizing highly and lifting up older people and putting them on a pedestal. A society that denigrates the elderly is a society with neither a past nor a future; it is society stuck in the meaningless moment of the present.

There is a Grimm's fairy tale of an old man who shook and trembled. He made a mess of things whenever he ate, usually getting more food on his clothes and the floor than into his mouth. One day, his fastidious daughter-in-law took the old man to the corner of the kitchen, sat him on a stool and placed an earthenware bowl in front of him. The old man, trembling a bit more than usual, accidentally knocked the bowl to the floor, where it shattered into pieces. The daughter-in-law said angrily, "If you're going to act like a pig, then I'm going to feed you out of a trough like a pig." So from that day on, she put his food into a wooden trough.

The old man's son and daughter-in-law had a small son whom they adored. One day the little boy was playing with bits and pieces of wood. "What are you doing?" his father asked. A smile creased his face as the little boy said, "Oh, I'm making a trough so I can take care of you and Mommy when you get old and I get big." Looking painfully at each other, the son and his wife walked over to the old man and gently led him back to the table, sat him on a chair, and placed a plate before him. The old man lived and ate as part of the family ever after.

"Honor your father and your mother." Put them on a pedestal! Remember, you owe your life to them. You were not manufactured; as the Bible puts it, you were begotten!

Remember! Remember your roots! Oliver Sacks wrote about Jimmie G., "He was a man without roots. . . . How could he connect?"[3] What is life without connections? Without roots we have no sense of history, no genealogy to claim, no cultural heritage to embrace. Roots connect, roots nourish, roots give us a center out of which to locate our lives in time and space.

I was a sophomore in high school when I earned my first varsity letter. With pride sticking out all over, I went into Portman's Sporting Goods store to order my first letter sweater. As I was being measured, the store owner came up to talk. When I told him my name, he immediately replied, "Oh, you must be Jerry's boy." I blushed and quickly tried to change the subject. Jerry was my father; he had been active in local politics, and most people knew who he was. But my parents had divorced and Jerry had left town with another woman. For the next fifteen years or so, I tried to ignore those roots.

One morning I awakened to the realization that, indeed, I was Jerry's boy. I bore his name, William Gerald Enright Jr. I had been blessed with some of his gifts. You can't disconnect from your past. You can't erase those chapters of your life that embarrass or wound you. You can't forget. There is always someone who will remember or someone who will innocently say something that will kick up dust from the past.

"Honor your father and your mother that your days may be long in the land." That last phrase is not so much a promise as it is just plain common sense. It is a reminder that actions have consequences. Roots both bless and wound; in the end, they exist to nourish us. Jean Illsley Clarke, in her book *Self-Esteem*, observes that "what families have in common the world around is that they are the place where people learn who they are."[4] Life goes best and we learn who we are when we take our roots seriously. Remember! Remember you are family! This Fifth Commandment is about family. Protestant, Catholic, Jew, Muslim, all agree: Family is the basic social institution. Take away the family and we become wanderers.

In recent decades, the continued decline of reverence for the family has become the root cause of "delinquency and crime, drug and alcohol abuse, suicide, depression, and eating disorders."[5]

What makes the Bible so believable is that it speaks with candor. What makes these channel markers so relevant is that they highlight reality. The family as portrayed in the Bible is very fragile if not downright dysfunctional. The family revealed is a family frayed by infidelities and feisty feuds and untimely deaths. Yet the family survives, not by its own doing but because of God's faithfulness fleshed out in grace and forgiveness, tolerance, and a pesky sense of promise keeping.

The family as described in the first book of the Bible, Genesis, makes the point. In Genesis 1, Adam is the apple of God's eye. By chapter 3, Adam has become, as they say, rotten to the core, and endangers all of God's pristine creation. In chapter 4, a sibling rivalry between Cain and Abel results in Abel's murder. Chapters 5 through 9 tell the story of Noah, who in spite of his faith and daring appears to have had a problem with alcohol. The saga of the family does not get better. Chapters 12 through 25 regale us with the episodes surrounding Abraham and Sarah who, in their chase of God's dream, scheme, lie, steal, and put themselves in what today we would call "sexually compromising situations!"

With chapter 25, a second sibling rivalry takes the stage in the form of twin brothers, Esau and Jacob. Esau, the older, is a hairy outdoorsman. Jacob, whose name means "trickster," is fair-skinned and domestic. Cultural protocol promises everything to the older brother, Esau. Yet Jacob was not born to be second. Jacob, with the help of his mother, deceives his blind father, Isaac, and cheats Esau out of the family inheritance. Jacob then runs for his life. Ironically, in the chase of life, Jacob flourishes. He fathers twelve sons. Jacob's boys reflect his genes; their manners and morals are perhaps even a tad worse.

One day, some of the brothers wake up to the reality that Jacob has been playing favorites with his boys. Young Joseph is his special prize. So the older brothers lure Joseph into a trap, throw him into a well, then sell him to a passing caravan. Joseph becomes a slave in Egypt. The story line of Genesis takes a new turn, and the spotlight shines on Joseph. Joseph has some unique gifts, and, in time, the slave becomes a member of Pharaoh's cabinet—the secretary of agriculture. In the meantime, the brothers' fortunes change. Famine grips the land, and one day they find themselves standing before Pharaoh's secretary of agriculture begging for food. Of course, they don't have a clue who the secretary is, and a new round of scheming begins.

Genesis closes with the story of Jacob's reunion with his long lost son, Joseph. The story is revealing. Three generations of family are together for the first time: Jacob with his son he thought to have been killed and Joseph with his two sons, Manasseh and Ephraim. Joseph named his firstborn son Manasseh, for the name means "forget it," and that is exactly what Joseph wanted to do with his past. The second son Joseph named Ephraim, which means "fruitful" or "flourish," for Joseph was now ready to live life to the full in his new land.

The old trickster Jacob wants to bless his two new grandsons. It is a holy moment, and protocol is very clear. First, he is to lay his right hand on the head of the older boy, then his left hand on the head of the younger boy. As Jacob reaches out, he suddenly crosses his hands. It is an inexcusable faux pas, like using the wrong name at a funeral or a wedding. "No, no, no," Joseph says as he reaches out to help the old man get his hands right. But Jacob resists, saying, "I know, my son, I know what I'm doing," as he proceeds to give the greater blessing to the younger boy, Flourish, at the expense of the older boy, Forget It. We cannot flourish if we are intent on forgetting the past.

Recently I attended a play titled *An Almost Holy Picture.* Samuel, a former Episcopal priest, now serves as the groundskeeper for the Church of the Holy Comforter. His life has been a standing argument with God. His little girl, Ariel, has been cursed with a rare disease that leaves her with hair on her face and body. Kids at school call her the "missing link" and "gorilla." Every week, her parents shave her body to make her more presentable, except during summers, which they spend on Cape Cod. One summer at the Cape, Ariel befriends an autistic boy, Angel, who has a flair for light and darkness and photography. For the first time, Ariel feels special. The boy's photographs are displayed in a gallery. Samuel and Ariel attend the opening. On the drive to the gallery, hairy little Ariel says, "Dad, guess what? I'm a princess."

When they arrive, Samuel is taken aback, infuriated by what he sees. The photographs are of his little girl: swimming nude in the bay, sitting nude on a blanket eating blackberries, sleeping nude in the woods, dancing nude by the sea. The pictures are in no way pornographic, for while Ariel is naked, she is always clothed by the shimmering halo of her golden hair swaddling her body. Still, the revelation of Ariel having been photographed without her clothes is more than Samuel can tolerate. Staggering forward, Samuel rips the photographs from the wall and runs from the gallery. Samuel and Ariel drive home, he in silent fury. Ariel is tear-stained and brokenhearted, embarrassed and no longer feeling like a princess.

Weeks pass; summer comes and goes. Samuel is back digging in his garden when that strange duet called guilt and grace begin to play their music in his soul. The hole Samuel is digging takes the shape of a grave. Into the hole Samuel throws some items which, as he puts it, "my daughter doesn't need me to do for her anymore." Finally come the photographs. Samuel says, "The bishop says there is a relation-

ship between our pain and our call. Love is a kind of voca-
tion that calls us to hard things. . . . My wife and my daughter, they call me . . . and I go toward the things I love."

Samuel takes the photographs; he is about to toss them
into the hole when he pauses, changing his mind. Pressing
the pictures of his naked but scarred daughter to his chest, he
says, "This one photograph with the white radiance of eternity emerging from the darkness was made for us. . . . It is, I
have come to believe, an almost holy picture." That's God's
family isn't it? An almost holy picture! Sacred but scarred.
Pocked with holes, yet holy.[6]

God has bet his world on the family. We survive as a family, not because of our own moral goodness but because of
God's irresistible grace and astonishing faithfulness. The
channel marker reads, Remember! Remember your parents!
Remember your roots! Remember, you are family!

Of course, you and I don't *have* to remember. These channel markers are only for those who want to partner their lives
with God and live in this new millennium with a difference.

Chapter 5

Reverence: The Sixth and Seventh Commandments

You shall not kill. You shall not commit adultery.

—Ex. 20:13–14

"*E*arly this morning, 1 January 2021, three minutes after midnight, the last human being to be born on earth was killed in a pub brawl in a suburb of Buenos Aires, aged twenty-five years, two months and twelve days. . . . Joseph Ricardo died as he had lived." With that riveting sentence, the British writer P. D. James begins her novel *The Children of Men.* She describes a world in which, overnight, the human race has lost its power to breed. Twenty-six years have passed since a baby was born. In the meantime, sex has become meaningless and violence commonplace, with outlaw bands of hopeless youth roving the landscape while mass government-assisted suicides relieve the old and the lame of the burden of living. The world P. D. James describes is, in her words, a world in which "science has been god." Now science is dead and humanity is doomed.[1]

Think about our world. Do not meaningless sex and commonplace violence also frame the headlines of our days? On prime-time television, the title character in *Frasier* finally goes out with the woman who, years earlier, had been homecoming queen at his high school. Later Frasier gloats to his psychiatrist brother, "I invited her for dinner and she stayed for breakfast." The bedroom scene between dinner and breakfast was no big deal, for, in our society, sex has become banal.

In a television documentary, *The Virus of Violence,* produced by a member of my congregation, Tom Cochrun, I learned that most children will witness two hundred thousand violent acts on television by the time they are eighteen years of age.[2] Thanks to violent video games, movies, and television, including the evening news, we are all desensitized as murder and adultery are portrayed as part of everyday life.

Several years ago, amidst the breaking Clinton sex scandal, a journalist was interviewing Robert George, professor of political philosophy at Princeton. The journalist expressed shock that, according to an NBC/*Wall Street Journal* poll, 66 percent of the American people did not care. He asked, "How could so many shrug off such charges?" George replied, "It's because we've lost a sense of the sacredness of life." "No, no, no," the reporter protested, "I'm not talking about abortion; I'm talking about adultery." George answered, "Both derive from the same worldview. Modern secular orthodoxy splits the human being, dividing the person from the body. The body is treated as an instrument for getting what the self wants—pleasure, emotional satisfaction, etc."[3]

Sex and violence bring us eyeball to eyeball with the Sixth and Seventh Commandments: "You shall not kill" and "You shall not commit adultery." These two commandments belong together. The channel marker behind them blinks the same message: Reverence! Where there is no reverence, no sense of the sacredness of life and the holiness of the body, sex becomes meaningless and violence commonplace. Of all the commandments, these two may be the most relevant for the new millennium.

Reverence has to do with honoring the body. It reflects the Judeo-Christian conviction that our bodies are made in the image of God. The old storytellers in Genesis 1 and 2 phrased it this way:

> Then God said, "Let us make humankind in our image. . . .
>
>> So God created humankind in his image,
>> in the image of God he created them;
>> male and female he created them. . . .
>
> . . . [T]hen the LORD God formed man from the dust of the ground, and breathed into his nostrils the breath of life; and the man became a living being.

The story sends shivers shooting through my being every time I read it. God did not create us as souls and then wrap a disposable body around us, as if to say that the body isn't important. No, God created the body, then brought the body to life by breathing his very presence into it. When it comes to honoring the body, biological life cannot be split off and separated from spiritual identity. We are persons who carry God's identity in our very being. Male and female together reflect the image of God. We exist to mirror God's presence in all our relationships: our speaking and our listening, our living and our loving.

In her book *For the Time Being,* Annie Dillard describes an uneducated southern preacher speaking to a revival crowd in Scottsboro, Alabama. Brother Carl Porter says, "God ain't no white-bearded old man up in the sky somewhere." The audience shouts back, "Amen! Thank God." Brother Carl continues, "He's a spirit. He ain't got no body. The only body he's got is us!" As the audience erupts into shouts of "Amen," Dillard comments, "That's a fine piece of modern theology: *the only body he's got is us!*"[4]

Reverence! There is something sacred about the body. God's presence lives in our bodies. These twin commandments read, "Don't kill; don't sleep around." A new Presbyterian catechism asks this question: "What do you learn from this commandment?" Answer: "I should honor every human being, including my enemy, as a person made in God's image."[5] Jesus understood the sacredness of the body. That is why Jesus gave an unexpected twist to these two commandments, equating abusive speech and behavior with murder and pornography with adultery (Matt. 5:21–30).

To me, this channel marker called reverence is more like a flashing yellow light than a stop and go traffic light alternating between red and green. The purpose of reverence is to give us pause rather than to arbitrarily bring us to a screeching stop or blindly propel us full speed ahead. It's a blinking yellow light, which means be careful, go slowly, beware of dangerous currents, proceed with caution. As we make our way through the rough waters of everyday living, reverence in the form of discernment is the key to survival. Don't kill! Don't sleep around! Your physical body and that of every human being around you are sacred; so live *reverence!*

I think of the flashing yellow light in times of war. John Calvin said that even in a just war, those who take life are "soiled . . . polluted before God."[6] In the Middle Ages, those who participated in a war "were required, at the war's end, not to march through the streets proud and victorious but to fall on their knees in penance and confession before they could partake of the Eucharist."[7] Reverence for life!

Bring up the subject of abortion and I am conscious of the blinking yellow channel marker. A professor at the UCLA medical school confronted his students with this case: "A father has syphilis; the mother has tuberculosis. They already have had four children. The first is blind, the second is dead, the third is deaf, the fourth also has tuberculosis. The mother is pregnant again. The parents are willing to have an abortion if you say they should. What do you advise?" The majority of students advised abortion. The professor said, "Congratulations, you have just killed Beethoven!"[8] Reverence for life!

That terrible modern disease called AIDS sets off this flashing channel marker. Imagine yourself as a Christian missionary in Africa where AIDS is now an epidemic. Some African nations may lose 20 percent of their population in the next few years as it is estimated that the annual AIDS death rate worldwide will be five million. In Botswana, life expectancy has plummeted from 65 in 1996 to 47 in 1999. In Kenya, a predominantly Christian nation, half of the young people who attend church are sexually active. Nearly one-third of the church leaders in Kenya have had sex outside of marriage. How do you talk about sex to people in this setting? Do you simply say, "Don't do it!" Writing in the conservative journal *Christianity Today,* Debbie Dortzbach, a twenty-seven-year missionary with World Relief, says, "We have to talk about the condom!" Why? Because "Christ as Lord of the church has not given up on his bride." Reverence for life![9]

The yellow light flashes whenever we debate the merits of capital punishment. The death sentence is one way by which our legal system pursues justice. Yet, in recent years, the miracle of DNA coupled with hard-nosed sociological research has revealed the fact that many inmates on death row are innocent of the crimes for which they await execution. This led George Ryan, the governor of the state of Illinois and a believer in capital punishment, to order a moratorium on all executions by the state.

The turbulent waters of biogenetics have also set the yellow light blinking. Gene therapy promises hope to all of us. We all carry defective genes. A young woman by the name of Christine DeMark has a mother with Huntington's disease. Christine took the test to determine her genetic vulnerability and the test came back positive. Today, Christine is in good health. However, because of the test, her fiancé has left her, her employer fired her, and no insurance company will have anything to do with her. Biogenetics can be a curse as well as a blessing. That is why President Clinton signed an order barring federal agencies from using genetic information in hiring. Sometimes the risks to human life do not justify the experiment. Recently, Beth Israel Hospital in Boston shut down its gene therapy program for the time being.[10]

Here are another pair of flashing yellow lights amidst the troubling currents of life: artificial insemination and surrogate motherhood. To be sure, artificial insemination is a precious gift, blessing otherwise hopeless couples with children. Yet when the donor of the sperm turns out to be a close family friend, as has happened, whose child is it? And what do you say to the woman who, having hired out her womb for a price, has trouble giving up the baby she produces? Reverence has to do with taking the time to ponder and anticipate the consequences of our actions.

Every time you go out on a date and ponder your appropriate sexual behavior, the yellow light is flashing. William Willimon, dean of the chapel at Duke University, tells this story. He had been speaking at a conference on evangelism in the Episcopal Church. Following his address, a young man came to talk with him. He told Willimon about a young woman he had met in California. They were on their first date. It went well. Toward the end of the evening she said, "Well, do you want to go to your place or mine?" "What are you talking about?" he asked. "You know," she said. "Don't you find me attractive?" "Of course," he replied, "but this is our first date! I hardly know you. We can't sleep together." "But I always sleep with guys on the first date," she responded. "I don't do that!" he said. "Why don't you?" she asked. "Because . . . um . . . um . . . um . . . I'm an Episcopalian," he stammered. "We're funny about who we sleep with." "Episcopalian. What's that?" she asked. "Well, it's a kind of a Christian," he answered. He then told her about his church. She was fascinated. He invited her to visit with him. She did. Three weeks later she asked the priest to baptize her. Willimon reflects on this story: "These days, just one person running loose in southern California who keeps the sixth commandment is enough to attract a crowd. Call it ordinary folk like us getting to be saints."[11]

Reverence! "You shall not kill! You shall not commit adultery." Behind those two commandments sits this Christian conviction: If you want to live life whole, you can never separate biology from theology or physiology from spirituality. Saint Paul believed that, for he wrote, "Your body is a temple of the Holy Spirit" (1 Cor. 6:19). The British physicist and theologian John Polkinghorne also believes that: "Religion without science is confined; it fails to be completely open to reality. Science without religion is incomplete; it fails to attain the deepest possible understanding."[12] Separate biology from theology and you get what the fifteenth-century theologian Nicholas of Cusa called "learned ignorance." Learned ignorance is truncated knowledge; it is knowing a lot about this but next to nothing about that.[13]

Why is it that some young people I know who have been burned in the bedroom are now committing themselves to abstinence until they marry? Because they cannot divorce physiology from spirituality, biology from theology. In casual sex, our bodies become trash to be thrown away.

Why is it that Colonel David Grossman, a West Point instructor who, for twenty-five years, trained people to kill, says that "killing is naturally repulsive? Because we humans possess an innate resistance to killing." Soldiers must be *trained* to kill! In World War II, only 15 percent of all combat soldiers were able to shoot to kill. Tragically, we have become more adept at training people to kill. In the Korean War, the figure was 55 percent, and by the time of Vietnam it was 90 percent. Separate theology from biology and we become diminished persons.[14]

Reverence! The last half of the aforementioned P. D. James novel, *The Children of Men,* is subtitled "Alpha"; it's the story of birth and a new beginning. There are five people who form a resistance movement. The Five adopt a logo, the fish. There is Theo, an aging Oxford history don, Miriam, a rusty midwife, Luke, an ineffectual old line Anglican priest, a young woman named Julian who is also a Christian, and Rolf, her husband. Wonder of wonders, Julian becomes pregnant, shockingly Luke is the father. Instantly the Five are thrown into a quandary over how to handle this scandalous miracle. Given the violent nature of society, they fear Julian may be hunted down and killed. Theo thinks otherwise. He wants Julian to go public with an announcement trumpeting, "This child belongs to mankind." Luke's protest wins the day as he shouts, "No! This child belongs to God!"[15]

Months pass. Julian has her baby in an abandoned rural shed, but birth has come with a price. Rolf has died. Both Luke and Miriam were killed protecting Julian and her unborn fetus. Once the child is born, Julian whispers, "Christen the baby for me. It's what Luke would have wanted; it's what I want." So the novel ends as Theo, recalling from his child-hood the rite of Baptism, with a thumb wet with tears and blood, makes on the child's forehead the sign of the cross.[16]

We are all God's children. We too bear on our foreheads the sign of the cross. Every day we must choose how we shall live: reverently or selfishly. Sadly, reverence does not become everyone. Reverence is only for those who want to partner their lives with God and live with a difference in this new millennium.

Chapter 6

Manners: The Eighth, Ninth, and Tenth Commandments

You shall not steal. You shall not bear false witness against your neighbor. You shall not covet . . . anything that belongs to your neighbor.

—Ex. 20:15–17

 is name was Henderson. As Saul Bellow tells the story, he had a legacy that left most people drooling. He was the multimillionaire son of a world famous scholar, the great-grandson of a secretary of state. His family was nearly as rich in ambassadorships as it was in money. He himself held two degrees from an Ivy League university and a Purple Heart from the war in North Africa and Sicily. Yet, by his own admission, Henderson's soul was "like a pawn shop . . . filled with unredeemed pleasures, old clarinets, cameras, and moth-eaten fur."[1] As Henderson describes himself,

> There was a disturbance in my heart, a voice that spoke there and said, "*I want, I want, I want!*" It happened every afternoon, and when I tried to suppress it, it got stronger. It said only one thing, "*I want, I want!*"
>
> And I would ask, "What do you want?" It never said a thing except "*I want, I want, I want!*" . . . At times I would treat it like an ailing child to whom you offer rhymes or

candy. I would walk it. I would trot it. I would sing to it. No use. . . . No purchase, no matter how expensive would lessen it. . . . The demand became only louder, "*I want, I want, I want, I want, I want!*"[2]

Most of us have heard that same voice from deep within ourselves. Because we *want,* we *steal*! We steal money, we steal things, we steal property, we steal ideas. We plot, we scheme, we deceive, we cheat, either because we want something we can't get honestly or because we are too lazy to put in the work to get it honestly. Concerning the Eighth Commandment, John Calvin wrote,

> There are many kinds of thefts. One consists in violence, when another's goods are stolen by force. A second kind consists in malicious deceit, when they are carried off through fraud. Another lies in concealed craftiness, when people's goods are snatched from them by legal means. Still another lies in flatteries, when one is cheated of goods under the pretense of a gift.[3]

I want, I want, I want! Because we want, we lie, or as the Ninth Commandment phrases it, we bear false witness. We are masters when it comes to gossip and rumor and innuendo. In politics and in business we distort the truth as we slander and malign to get what we want. A recent Presbyterian catechism says, "God forbids me to damage the honor or reputation of my neighbor. I should not say false things against anyone . . . for any reason. God requires me to speak the truth . . . and to view the faults of my neighbor with tolerance when I cannot."[4]

I want, I want, I want! Because we *want,* we *covet* what other people have. We resent the good fortune of a neighbor in the stock market. We become jealous when a colleague gets a promotion or a higher pay raise. We grow envious of friends who move into new homes or send their kids to private schools and colleges. Writing on the Tenth Commandment, Stanley Hauerwas and William Willimon observe, "We have managed to blacken our mirrors so that we no longer see ourselves."[5]

I want, I want, I want! Again and again our wants land us bare-bottomed in the briar patch of the Eighth, Ninth, and Tenth Commandments: "You shall not steal. You shall not bear false witness against your neighbor. You shall not covet . . . anything that belongs to your neighbor."

Remember, these commandments are not intended to serve so much as legal absolutes and rigid moral imperatives as they are channel markers to guide us in our living together as children of God. The channel marker reflecting the intent of these three commandments simply reads: Mind your manners!

Ironically, that is what my mother used to say to me as a boy when I did not behave properly in public. "William, mind your manners!" "You never address older people by their first names!" "You always open the door for a lady!" "You never speak critically of other people in public." Manners!

Stephen Carter, professor of law at Yale, calls manners "the etiquette of democracy." Among the rules of etiquette Carter cites as essential to our social well-being are these:

> Our duty to be civil toward others does not depend upon whether we like them or not.
> Civility requires that we sacrifice for strangers, not just for people we happen to know.
> Civility has two parts: generosity, even when it is costly, and trust, even when there is risk.
> Civility creates not merely a negative duty not to do harm, but an affirmative duty to do good.
> Civility requires that we express ourselves in ways that demonstrate our respect for others.[6]

Mind your manners! "You shall not steal." The manner behind that commandment is this: Respect what belongs to others. Take away respect and we lose all sense of community as chaos sets in. To survive in the human community, persons need things to own, and persons have a right to own those things they need. Theft is an attack on the dignity and well-being of another person. People who have been robbed use the same word in describing their feelings to me; they say, "I felt violated!" Thievery violates a person because our identity is related to what we possess. John Calvin observed that this Eighth Commandment was more than a prohibition; it was an obligation. It obligates us to care for others' good or well-being.[7]

Ah, but there is a thief in most of us. Our wants get in the way of our respect for what belongs to others. Years ago, the thief in me caught me by surprise high on a ridge in the Himalayas. I was in India and Nepal on a mission tour, and my doctor friend and I had taken a day off to hike in the mountains for a clearer view of Mount Everest. As we were walking along a narrow path with our guide, a Nepali boy came up to me and offered me a knife. He wanted ten dollars for it. I shrugged my shoulders and walked away, as I was not interested in buying a knife. The boy followed saying, "All right, give me five dollars." I paused to examine the knife more closely. It was an extraordinary knife, hand carved, fiercely curved, and neatly tucked into a black leather sheath. As knives go, it was just the kind of souvenir that would make a wonderful conversation piece on a book shelf or mantel. I thought to myself, "This knife is worth more than five or ten dollars." I turned and said to the boy, "I'll give you one dollar." Insulted, he stomped away. The knife belonged to him; it was something he owned. I was also aware that I had him over a barrel because he wanted American dollars. A hundred yards down the trail the boy returned. I bought the knife for one dollar.

For the record, I paid for the knife. For the record, I also violated the Eighth Commandment; I stole that knife. Trying to get something for nothing, failing to pay a fair price for what belongs to another, taking advantage of a situation— we've all done that, haven't we? Manners have to do with respecting what belongs to others.

Mind your manners! "You shall not bear false witness against your neighbor." It is not enough to respect what *belongs* to others; manners also have to do with respecting the person. When we respect a person, we speak truthfully about that person.

There is a relationship between the secular notion of civility and the Christian ideal of awe. It is a Judeo-Christian conviction: Humans are persons who have been made in the image of God. Consequently, when I enter into the presence of another person, I enter into the presence of God. When we speak about or to another person, we speak with awe and humility. To lie about another person, to demean or put that person down, is to demean God.

In ancient Israel, the courtroom was located at the city gate. Justice was not something one chased down behind closed doors; justice was pursued out in the open where everyone could see and hear for himself or herself. In those days, you did not hire an attorney to defend you; you pled your own case, summoned your own witnesses, and acted as your own counsel. The judge listened, then rendered a verdict. With one dishonest witness, you could lose everything. Justice turned on the truthfulness of the witness. Manners have to do with respecting a person so much that we are always truthful in what we say about that person.

The historians of ancient Israel told this story. Once upon a time there lived a man named Naboth who owned a valuable vineyard located near the royal palace. On occasion, the king, whose name was Ahab, would wander out on his veranda, look at the surrounding countryside and dream about what he would do with the land if only it belonged to him. One day, the king noticed that Naboth was outside inspecting his vineyards, so the king decided to pay the man a visit. As they talked, the king made an offer. In exchange for the vineyard next to the palace the king would give to Naboth a larger and better vineyard located some distance away. Naboth was not interested in swapping vineyards. The king then offered to pay Naboth whatever price he wanted for the land. It was a fair offer. Naboth turned it down, saying that the vineyard had been in his family for generations. Rebuffed, King Ahab went home to pout. At dinner, King Ahab was still in a snit. As Queen Jezebel listened to her husband's story, she decided to take matters into her own hands. She secretly met with some of the movers and shakers of the city, and together they hatched a scam to frame and defame Naboth publicly by having two cronies charge him with disloyalty and insubordination to both the crown and to God. The upshot was that Naboth was executed as a criminal, freeing Ahab to claim the land.

That story, as found in 1 Kings 21, might have ended then and there. Curiously, the real story begins where it should have ended. The prophet Elijah hears of the injustice and is infuriated. He calls King Ahab and Queen Jezebel to account and informs them that, because of their behavior, their days on the throne are numbered. What's the point of the story? In God's scheme of life, manners do matter; truth counts, and in the end justice prevails!

Mind your manners! "You shall not covet anything that belongs to your neighbor." The manner behind the Tenth Commandment simply reads, Watch out for your wants! Covetousness has to do with those insatiable drives and desires that live deep within us. Greed, lust, and ambition are the stuff on which covetousness feeds. Covetousness is the name we give to those dark wants that rumble around within us. Covetousness is that revved up engine inside us that pushes us onto the fast track of life. To survive, we need to mind our manners by keeping an eye on our wants and listening to our hearts.

The first nine of the Ten Commandments have to do with behavior. The Tenth Commandment points to our hearts as it strikes at the motive behind our behavior. The only antidote to covetousness, says John Calvin, is the "heart steeped in love!" What is this commandment to teach us? The catechism answers, "That my whole heart should belong to God alone, not to money or the things of this world."[8]

Adam Smith, who has been called the "father of capitalism," was an eighteenth-century Scot. For a time, he was dean of the faculty and professor of moral philosophy at the University of Glasgow. Then he was offered a chance to become the tutor of the Duke of Buccleuch, who was but a small boy. For this, he was promised an annual pension of three hundred pounds sterling for the rest of his life. Because of his own financial needs, Smith resigned his post at the university. Years later, he was appointed the commissioner of customs in Scotland, a post that carried with it an annual salary of six hundred pounds sterling. Suddenly Adam Smith was no longer a man with financial needs. So he picked up his pen and wrote the Duke of Buccleuch, now a grown man, to tell him that he no longer needed his annual pension as "he now had more than enough."[9]

How did Adam Smith know when enough was enough? He kept an eye on his wants. He believed that deep within each of us there exists a voice. He called this voice the "impartial spectator" whose business it is to monitor our wants and our behavior.[10]

I want, I want, I want! Because of that voice, at age fifty-five, Henderson, in Bellow's novel, bought a ticket and flew halfway around the world to Africa. In his trek across that continent, he struck up a friendship with a wise tribal king. Henderson told the African king about the voice that sounded within him each day saying, "I want, I want, I want!" In time, Henderson learned this from the king about that voice: Our wants are always illusory. The more we have, the more we want. Things cannot satisfy that voice sounding from deep within, for what the voice is seeking is not material things, but reality—greatness—God! The voice inside is there to witness to the fact that "the universe itself has been put into us . . .the eternal bonded onto us."[11]

The voice crying from somewhere deep within you, "I want, I want, I want!" doesn't have anything to do with things and the accumulation of things, for in the end it is not our neighbor's house, our neighbor's wealth, or our neighbor's spouse we covet; it is God we covet. The voice is our starved soul crying for God.

And that is the genius of these ten channel markers. The genius of the Ten Commandments is not that God gave them. The genius of these channel markers is that when we take them seriously and follow them, something surprising happens to us. We find ourselves living life in the presence of God because they exist to reveal God to us. This is why I have repeated that these channel markers are not for everyone. They are only for those who want to partner their lives with God and live with a difference in this new millennium!

PART 2 The Sermon on the Mount

Chapter 7

Heading for the Open Sea

You shall love the Lord your God with all your heart,
and with all your soul, and with all your mind,
and with all your strength. . . . You shall
love your neighbor as yourself.

—Mark 12:30–31

n Herman Melville's classic story *Moby Dick,* Ishmael, a schoolteacher, decides to abandon the security of the classroom for the adventure of the sea. Why? Because that is how Ishmael cares for his soul or, as he puts it, "drives off the spleen." He muses,

> Whenever I find myself growing grim about the mouth; whenever it is a damp, drizzly November in my soul. . . . It's time to get to the sea as soon as I can. . . . Almost all men, some time or other, cherish . . . the same feelings toward the ocean with me. . . . When I go to sea, I go as a simple sailor, right before the mast. . . . I love to sail forbidden seas and land on barbarous coasts.[1]

In the previous chapters of the book, I have written about the Ten Commandments as channel markers. The first two commandments have to do with priorities. Living in such a way as to put God first: "You shall have no other gods before me. You shall not make for yourself an idol."

The Third Commandment is a call to integrity. We are challenged to live out our faith on the public squares of our world with savvy and integrity: "You shall not make wrongful use of the name of the LORD your God."

The fourth is about time. Taking the time to listen to the rhythms of life and honor the rituals of the soul so that we may live life whole: "Remember the sabbath day, and keep it holy."

The Fifth Commandment has to do with remembering our roots, remembering our parents, remembering we are family: "Honor your father and your mother."

The Sixth and Seventh Commandments belong together, for they both command reverence, reverence for life and reverence for the body of every human we touch: "You shall not kill. You shall not commit adultery."

The last three commandments are about manners. If we humans are going to learn to live together in community and harmony, we must mind our manners. We must respect what belongs to other people: "You shall not steal." We must respect other people as persons when we talk about them: "You shall not bear false witness against your neighbor." The final commandment reminds us that people with good manners keep a wary eye on their own wants: "You shall not covet anything that belongs to your neighbor."

The Ten Commandments give us six channel markers: priorities, integrity, time, memory, reverence, and manners. Here is the rub: Channel markers are found only in harbors and coastal shorelines or inland waterways. But in most of us there is an Ishmael, a person born to go to sea.

I think Jesus understood the lure of the sea and the deeper waters. In Luke 5, Jesus is standing along a beach, talking to people, when he spots two empty boats by the water's edge. Commandeering one of the boats, he tells a startled fisherman to push the boat out, a tad off shore, so he may use it as a pulpit to talk to the crowd. Once his talk is over, Jesus asks the fisherman, a blustery fellow named Simon Peter, to push out to the deeper water so they can fish. "Master," booms Simon, his voice roaring like a lion in a cave, "we've been fishing all night and have nothing to show for it." "All night?" Jesus asks. "Yeah!" replies Simon. "And you caught nothing?" Jesus asks. "That's right, nothing," snaps Simon as testiness throttles his voice. Then, like a comedian setting up a straight man, Jesus says, "And you do this for a living? This is what you're good at?"

Snarling, Simon silently sets his sail for the deeper waters as he angrily throws his fishing nets into the water. No sooner do the nets hit the water than the lake begins to boil. There are more fish than Simon and his partners can handle. Later, after they have hauled in the catch, Simon shoots a nervous glance at Jesus. Jesus is laughing and there is a twinkle in his voice as he says, "Simon, how would you like to spend your life at something you could really become good at—like fishing for people?"[2]

"Put out into the deep water," Jesus says. If Simon Peter, if we, are going to make our lives count for something, we must head for the open and deeper waters where the fish lurk, the sharks prey, and the dolphins play. The problem with oceans and deep waters is that they have no channel markers.

In an essay titled "Theology," C. S. Lewis describes a man standing on a beach looking at the Atlantic Ocean and studying a map of it. Lewis observes that such a man will not get anywhere by looking at maps. To go somewhere, the man must first go to sea. But, Lewis argues, once he decides to go to sea, he will not "be very safe without a map."[3]

What's the map to guide us when we leave the shelter of the inland waterways of life and take to the open sea? The map is what Jesus called the *Great Commandment*. It is what the Hebrew Scriptures call the *Shema*. It is what the catechisms of the church call the summation of the Ten Commandments: "You shall love the Lord your God with all your heart, and with all your soul, and with all your mind, and with all your strength. You shall love your neighbor as yourself."

The question is, how do we read this map? To love God with all our heart and soul and mind is to love God with our whole self, with our emotions and our passions, with our minds and our intelligence, with our goods and our material belongings. Our love of God is to shape how we do business, how we think about social and political issues, how we read history, how we address problems and resolve disputes, how we handle our finances.[4]

To love our neighbor as we love ourselves is to treat people as if we were walking in their shoes. How would you feel if you were poor? What would you want someone to say to you if you were living through the pain of a divorce? If you were a Muslim living in America, how would you want people who call themselves Christians to relate to you? If you were gay or lesbian, how would you want other people to talk about you? Imagine yourself as handicapped or disabled or elderly and arthritic in a culture that worships prime-time bodies. Love looks beyond appearances. Love sees through labels. Love gets involved because love cares. Love has both the discernment and the imagination to see the whole person within the wounded person, the complex person lashing out behind the angry person, the gifted person living encased in the flawed person.

It is, as C. S. Lewis once noted, "a serious thing" to live in a world where "there are no ordinary people." Because we all are made in the image of God, it is "immortals with whom we joke, work, marry, snub and exploit." Every person has the potential to be "an immortal horror" or an "everlasting splendor." "In some degree we help each other to one or another of these destinations."[5]

Recently I was invited to Washington to meet with the

president and tell the story of how some of us in Indianapolis are attempting to build bridges of faith, hope, and racial reconciliation in our city. For ten years I had been the pastor of one of the largest congregations in Indianapolis. Yet, I did not know, by more than name, any of my black brothers and sisters who were pastors of essentially African-American congregations. I decided to do something about that vacuum in my life. I began meeting monthly with the pastor of the then largest African-American congregation in our city, Bishop Tom Benjamin. We asked the rabbi of a large Hebrew congregation to join us. Our luncheon group began to grow as we included members from our respective congregations.

In time as our city became more sensitive to its own racial issues Bishop Benjamin and I were asked to co-chair a mayor's task force on racism. Out of that task force grew a plan for the city called *Vision Indianapolis*. At the same time we birthed a decidedly religious movement called *Celebration of Hope* which now numbers some forty congregations. Once a month we meet together as pastors for planning, dialogue, and prayer. We exchange pulpits with each other. Members from our respective congregations regularly meet in focus groups to build friendships and talk about issues which too often divide us.

We worship together. Once a year we close our respective church doors on Sunday morning in order to come together to celebrate our unity. We pair together as two or three congregations to engage in common mission projects and programs. As I sat in the East Room of the White House listening to others from around the nation share their stories I heard this text referred to on two different occasions in the space of less than an hour: "You shall love the Lord your God with all your heart, and with all your soul, and with all your mind, and with all your strength. You shall love your neighbor as yourself."

A rabbi from New York referred to this text, reminding us

that in the Hebrew language there is but one word for love. For the Jew, he said, there are no variations or gradations when it comes to love. In this world there are but two things: love and love's opposite! So when God said to love the Lord with all your heart, soul, mind, and strength, and your neighbor as yourself, God was saying something exceedingly important. We choose how we will live, this way or that!

The president also quoted our text as he walked us around our world from N. Ireland to Europe to Asia to Africa. As he came to one trouble spot after another he would pause, then, citing the tension, he would say, "Is the problem ethnic and racial or is it religious? I don't know." He concluded with our text, saying, "We all agree that we should love our neighbor as we love ourselves, but I need you, as religious leaders, to help us put that belief into action if we are going to live as one in our nation and world."

As I read the gospel story, Jesus Christ came to bring us together, not to tear us apart. As Saint Paul so eloquently phrased it, Christ "has broken down the dividing wall, that is, the hostility between us" (Eph. 2:14).

The question is, who is my neighbor? Do you remember how Jesus answered that question? He told the story of the Good Samaritan. What made the Samaritan good was what he did to someone he did not even know, someone who was of another religion and ethnic background. The Samaritan did not try to convert the fellow or discuss ethnic differences; he just did the right thing—he cared for the man.

Our neighbor is more than the person next door. Our neighbor is the Buddhist in China, the Muslim in Croatia, the Catholic in Ireland, the malnourished child in Mozambique, the AIDS victim in Kenya, the criminal on death row, the wealthy retiree in the Bahamas, the powerful CEO, and the jobless poor people in our cities. Jesus told that story to make this point: Our neighbor is everyone, everywhere!

G. K. Chesterton made this paradoxical observation: "The

person who lives in a small community lives in a much larger world. In a large community we can choose our companions. In a small community our companions are chosen for us." Philip Yancey, a contemporary writer, says, "Precisely! Given the choice I tend to hang out with folks like me. . . . [S]maller groups force me to rub shoulders with everybody else." Henri Nouwen defined community as "the place where the person you least want to live with always lives."[6]

Ironically, Chesterton wrote those words in defense of the family. He said that most people defend the family as that place where, amidst the stress and fickleness of life, we experience "life as peaceful, pleasant and at one." He continued: "There is another defense of the family which is to me evident: this is that the family is not peaceful and not pleasant and not at one." Loving God with your whole self and loving your neighbor as yourself begins on your own front porch.[7]

Stephen Carter, professor of law at Yale, tells this story. In the summer of 1966 his family moved to a large house in northwest Washington, D.C. It was a lily-white enclave of lobbyists, undersecretaries of this and that, and well-known senators. Stephen, one of five children, says that he and his siblings had never lived in a white neighborhood before, but that they had heard unpleasant rumors. So it was that moving day found the five Carter children sitting on the steps of their grand new house, wishing they were elsewhere. As they sat, their minds in the past, cars would pass, slow down, and drive on. People on foot did the same. Carter writes: "We waited for somebody to say, 'Hello,' but nobody did."

Then a white woman, arriving home from work at the house across the street, turned, smiled, and called out, "Welcome," before disappearing beyond the front door. Minutes later, she emerged from the same front door with a tray laden with cream cheese and jelly sandwiches that she carried across the street to the five children sitting on the steps. Then, with a ready smile, she greeted and fed each child. Carter writes, "Sara Kestenbaum was generous when nobody forced her to be, trusting when there was no reason to be, . . . creating for us a sense of belonging where none had existed before. . . . In the course of a single day she turned us from strangers into friends." Loving God with your whole self and loving your neighbor as yourself also begins in the neighborhood where you live.[8]

It's not easy sailing on the open seas. It's not easy unless you have a map to guide you. We have the map. What difference would it make if we took that map seriously? What if we genuinely loved God with our whole self and let that love shape our everyday living? What if we had just enough impish moxie to try to love all those squirrelly people around us just as they are? I believe that we would be stretched as we have never been stretched. We would also be blessed as we have never been blessed.

But then, these maps and channel markers are not for everyone. They are only for those who want to follow Jesus Christ in partnering their life with God and to live with a difference in this new millennium.

Chapter 8

Living as If

The kingdom of God is among you.
—Luke 17:21

A popular bumper sticker reads: "Christians aren't perfect, just forgiven!" Is forgiveness all there is to being a Christian? To be sure, Christians are not perfect, but is forgiveness what Christianity is all about?

Rasputin, a Russian mystic and scalawag who lived at the turn of the last century, thought so. Convinced that salvation was only for people who were good at sinning, Rasputin reduced the essence of Christianity to three terse sentences: "God loves to forgive! I love to sin! We have the perfect arrangement!"

Dallas Willard, chair of the department of philosophy at the University of Southern California, observes that many Christians have taken this story of Jesus we call *the gospel* and reduced it to a mere "bar-code faith" called forgiveness. You go to the supermarket and select whatever it is you want. Next you go to the checkout counter where the scanner responds only to the bar code. It does not matter what is in the package or bottle. The sticker on the item you purchased does not even have to be right. The electronic calculator responds only to the bar code. If you bought baby food and the sticker is for cat food, the scanner says that the baby food is cat food and that's that. So when you die, the only thing that matters to the great scanner in the sky is that the barcode reads: Forgiven! In such a system, how you live has little connection to being a Christian. Forgiveness, or the management of sins, is all that matters.[1]

A heretical thought begins to amble across my mind: What if the good news of Jesus Christ is not so much about sinning as it is about living? What if the essence of the Christian life is not forgiveness but discipleship? As I read my Bible, that is how Jesus understood the gospel. Jesus once described what he was all about this way. Jesus said, "I came that [you] may have life, and have it abundantly."

A disciple is a follower, an apprentice. A disciple is someone who wants to become what someone else is. Christians are people who want to be like Jesus and live as Jesus lived. Do you remember how Jesus described himself? He described himself as someone who was living in the kingdom of God. For Jesus, God's kingdom was as near as the tips of his fingers. What left people in awe around Jesus was this: Jesus treated the people he met as if they too were living in the kingdom of God.

C. S. Lewis once described Christians as people who "dress up as Christ": "The moment you realize 'Here I am, dressing up as Christ,' . . . you will see at once some way in which, at that very moment, the pretense could be made less of a pretense and more of a reality."[2] It is only as we pretend and imagine ourselves to be "little Christs" that everyday life begins to be transformed into meaning as, to borrow another phrase from Lewis, "the tin soldier" inside us begins to "turn into a living person."[3]

I believe that if we reduce Christianity to a bar code faith concerned only with sin management, God becomes both innocuous and irrelevant to everyday living. But, then, I am one of those strange Christians who calls himself a *Presby-*

terian. The word *Presbyterian* comes from the ancient Greek language and means "elder," or "old." It has something to do with wisdom, leadership, and good judgment. For Presbyterians, the Christian faith is supposed to be something you live as well as something you confess. John Calvin, who is to Presbyterians what Martin Luther is to Lutherans, said, "Rebirth in Christ does not take place in one moment or one day or one year." Calvin described the Christian life as a "race of repentance . . . run throughout our lives." Christians are people who try to live right and try to do things right because, by God's grace, they "aspire to a heavenly life."[4]

In the Bible, this aspiration to chase heaven and make it a reality here and now has a special name—the kingdom of God. Jesus put it this way: "The kingdom of God is among you." In other words, the kingdom of God is all around you, it is within you, it is at your fingertips. Christians are people who let their imaginations shape their living as they imagine themselves to be living in the kingdom of God right now. But what does it mean to live *as if* you were living in the kingdom?

Michael Murphy was on his way from California to India by way of Scotland. He wanted to pay his respects to a plot of land in Scotland called "The Kingdom." The Kingdom was located along the shore of the North Sea, sandwiched between the Firth of Forth and the Firth of Tay. The Kingdom is the birthplace of golf. So it was that Michael found himself standing on the first tee of this hallowed ground with a bucktoothed teaching pro named Shivas Irons and the man to whom Shivas was giving a lesson, Mr. MacIver. "Murphy," Shivas said as he gestured toward the tee, "hav' a try at the ball." As Michael bent over to tee up his ball, it suddenly dawned on him that he was in The Kingdom. As he stood to address the ball, nervousness so overtook him that he knocked the ball off the tee with the club face. Regaining his composure, he teed the ball up again and hit the ball clean and straight, far down the right side of the fairway. Michael put his second shot on the green, got down in two for a par and wrote "4" on his scorecard.

On the second hole, he hit another lovely drive. Alas, he pulled his second shot into an adjoining fairway and put his third shot into a deep bunker before blasting onto the green, where he two-putted for a double bogey. That is when Mr. MacIver volunteered to keep score. Michael protested, preferring to keep his own score, but MacIver insisted. "What did you have?" he asked. Michael replied, "Four on the first, and a six on the second." Turning, a stern look on his face, Shivas said, "Ye had a five oon the first. Ye must count that one ye knocked off the tee when ye took yer waggle. 'Tis the only way to play in The Kingdom."

Things went from bad to worse as Murphy hit his next tee shot into a patch of spiny shrubs called gorse. Eight shots later, his ball now pocked with large gashes, he reached the green, where it took him three putts to get down. "Murphy," MacIver asked, "how many?" Michael replied, "Just give me an X." "A what?" asked the puzzled scorekeeper. "I'm not counting the hole." Stepping in again, Shivas said, "Noo, Michael, put doon yer score; it'll do ye good." "OK, put down a ten," Michael responded. "Michael," Shivas interrupted, "Ah think 'twas eleven. . . . Remember, yer playin' in The Kingdom."

Slowly, a magical transformation began to take place in Michael's game. As Michael worked through his frustration, he began to relax and he listened in on what Shivas was saying to MacIver. He heard the old pro talking about something called "true gravity." True gravity, it seems, had to do with "just swingin' . . . with just letting the nothingness into yer shots . . . with seeing the flight of the ball in yer mind before ye swing . . . with imagining."

Several hours later, at the end of the eighteenth hole, Shivas, draping an arm around Michael's shoulder, said, "Ye deseruv' a drink. . . . Ye shot a 34 comin' in after a 52 goin' oot. True gravity works when you imagine golf as 'twas meant to be played in The Kingdom."[5]

To live as if we were in the kingdom is to imagine life as God wishes it to be. To live as if we were in the kingdom of God raises the bar on the quality of our living and our behavior.

In what tradition calls "the Sermon on the Mount" (Matt. 5–7), Jesus talks about what it means to live as if we were living in the kingdom of God. Near the beginning of that sermon, Jesus says, "You are the salt of the earth. . . . You are the light of the world." Jesus does not say, "You should be" or "You can be." He says, "You are"! You are in the kingdom now; live like it! Matthew's point is this: The church exists to live the kingdom life in the world!

When Jesus looked at life, he saw something special—he saw a God-bathed world. To live as if the kingdom were here is to live open to God's surprises. The largest church in the world is in Seoul, Korea. The pastor, Paul Cho, grew up as a Buddhist. As a young man dying of tuberculosis, he heard that "the God of the Christians" healed people. He prayed for God to help him and God did! In a God-bathed world, coincidences happen.

There is a man who attends my church every Sunday. Last month over lunch he told me this story. Five years ago he was an atheist. Then, one night while standing in his vast library, he felt himself surrounded by a presence. It was not visible, yet it was too tangible to be written off as a mere sensation or feeling. He said, "That night I knew for certain there was a God, for I experienced God's presence." A God-bathed world is a world of happenings beyond words.

A God-bathed world is a world which cannot shut out God. Jesus lived as if God were lurking around every corner, waiting just over the next hill, hiding behind every face, ready to speak through every one of his words. Remember how Jesus phrased it: "The kingdom of God is among you." "You are the salt of the earth. . . . You are the light of the world." In other words, live as if the kingdom is at your fingertips. Pretend you are in it now!

Living as if you were in the kingdom is more like painting a portrait than like following a set of rules. It is as if, looking into a mirror, you see yourself "dressed as Christ" and decide to try to live as you look in the mirror.

Take care, because living as if you were in the kingdom will stretch you. A professor at Texas A&M University gave her students an assignment to write a short essay on the Sermon on the Mount. This is what some of her students wrote:

> "In my opinion religion is one big hoax."
> "There is an old saying that 'You shouldn't believe everything you read' and it applies in this case."
> "The things asked in this sermon are absurd . . . the most extreme, stupid, unhuman statements that I have ever heard."

The professor, Virginia Stem Owens, says that, living in the Bible Belt, she expected her students to have respect for the text. Initially shocked by their response, she became heartened by what she read in their essays.

> I began to be encouraged. There is something exquisitely innocent about not realizing you shouldn't call Jesus stupid. . . . This was the real thing, a pristine response to the gospel, unfiltered through a two-millennia cultural haze. . . . I find it strangely heartening that the Bible remains offensive to honest, ignorant ears, just as it was in the first century. For me, that validates its significance.[6]

To be certain, there is something chilling about this Sermon on the Mount with its stern idealisms; living as if the kingdom is here can leave you looking the fool. Jesus would say it can even get you killed. But then, as Paul wrote to the first Christians in Corinth, what the world calls savvy and wise, God calls foolish. And what God considers smart, the world writes off as stupid, but only for the time being.

Why is it that history has never been able to write off Jesus of Nazareth? I suggest that it is because Jesus knew how to live. There was never anyone who was quite like him. Jesus lived as if God were at his fingertips. Jesus made God's presence in our world as real as a hungry beggar, a child's fever, a catch of fish, a toast at a wedding, a severed ear, one neighbor helping another, a dead man walking.

Jesus said, "You are the salt of the earth. . . . You are the light of the world." "The kingdom of God is in your midst." Live as if God is at your fingertips. Such living will stretch us, but never will it undo us. Read carefully this Sermon on the Mount. It talks about a kingdom where everyone is equal: "murderers and temper-throwers, adulterers and lusters, thieves and coveters," secular humanists and religious hypocrites.[7]

When Jesus said to live as if God is at our fingertips, he was raising the bar on life. God's ideal is something we never stop chasing. As for failure, our never measuring up? Hah! When we fail, we simply join the rest of humanity in the safety net of God's amazing and absolute grace—which leaves us free to live *as if* again!

Chapter 9

Living as if the World
Were a Safe Place

Do not worry about your life.
—Matt. 6:25

*W*hat makes a leader? Amidst the craze we call
"March Madness," I'm watching a lot of basketball games these days. It's the last few minutes of a close game that intrigue me. Come
crunch time, when the game is on the line, how is it that a
gifted athlete fizzles while an athlete with more modest tal-
ent rallies his or her team to victory?

Every businessperson knows a story about a highly intel-
ligent and extraordinarily skilled executive who, once promoted into a leadership position, fails at the job. He or she
also knows a story about someone with solid, but not extraordinary, gifts and skills who, when promoted into a similar
position, soars! What makes for the right stuff when it comes
to living and leadership?

Jesus had an answer to that question. He said it was living
as if this world were a safe place. Jesus never allowed his
fears and anxieties to inhibit and undo him.

In 1998, Daniel Goleman wrote an essay in the *Harvard
Business Review* in which he said that the secret to effective
leadership had to do with what he called "EQ," or emotional
intelligence. That article became the highest reader-rated

article in the history of the *Harvard Business Journal*. EQ has five components:

> *Self-awareness*: the ability of individuals to recognize their own moods and emotions and the way they affect everyone around them.
>
> *Self-regulation*: the ability of individuals to control their disruptive impulses and think before acting.
>
> *Motivation*: a passion to excel for reasons beyond money or status.
>
> *Empathy*: the ability to understand and respect the emotional makeup of other people.
>
> *Social skill*: proficiency in managing relationships and finding common ground.[1]

In a recent interview, Goleman called Jesus the "model of remarkable emotional intelligence."[2]

Jesus exuded emotional and spiritual intelligence because he allowed his imagination to shape his living. He lived as if the kingdom of God were all around him. He lived as if God were always at his fingertips. He lived as if heaven were here on earth. He lived as if strangers were persons to be welcomed and embraced rather than shunned or feared. In short, Jesus lived as if this world were a safe place!

In the Sermon on the Mount, Jesus raises the bar on human behavior by challenging us to live as if we too were in the kingdom. To live as if we were in the kingdom is to live as if this world were a safe place. Jesus put it this way: "Do not worry about your life!"

Some years ago Peter Gomes, professor of Christian morals and preacher to Harvard University, used this text from Matthew in a commencement address at a very posh girls' school in Manhattan. At a reception following the commencement, the father of one of the girls came up to Gomes with fire in his eyes and ice in his voice, saying, "That was

nonsense. Do not be anxious about your life!" Gomes told
the man that those were not his words but the words of Jesus.
The man replied, "It's still nonsense. It was anxiety that got
my daughter into this school, it was anxiety that kept her
here, it was anxiety that got her into Yale, it will be anxiety
that will keep her there, and it will be anxiety that will get her
a good job. You are selling nonsense."[3]

Is it nonsense to live as if we were in the kingdom, with
God no further away than our fingertips? How do you handle
your anxieties? Common street wisdom says that the best
hedge against insecurity is the stockpiling of wealth and the
creation of a sanctuary in which we can live dependent on no
one. Jesus says that the problem with investing our security
and self-worth in money and possessions is this: They are
never safe. Cash can be stolen. Securities can crash. Corpo-
rations can merge or collapse. Cadillacs have been known to
rust. Designer clothes provide moths with just another lus-
cious lunch. Security systems fail. In time, most of us retire.
Disease is blind to economic status. Later, if not sooner, death
comes to us all. In the meantime, in this kind of world, Jesus
says that there is only one way to live and make life count for
something. We are to live as if this world were a safe place![4]

What about our anxieties? All of us have sweated exams
we had to pass. All of us have endured interviews with our
futures in the balance. Most of us have had times when our
bills exceeded our income. We all know the agony of trying
to balance a checkbook on a limited budget. None of us is a
stranger to disappointment. All of us have suffered through
illnesses. Yet here we sit, our hearts beating and our minds
alert!

Read this paraphrase of Matthew 6:19–34 as if Jesus were
speaking to us today:

Don't be anxious about what is going to happen to you.
Don't worry about having enough money to pay your bills,

about food and clothes, about job security, about getting
your kids through college, about having enough money to
see you through retirement. Take a lesson from the birds of
the air. They don't hoard away in granaries, and your Father
sees that they have food. You are more important to God
than birds, aren't you? Stop your worrying!

Look at the flowers in the fields. They don't worry
about dress or style, yet their wardrobe is more stunning
than some of the "best dressed" people in the world. Now,
if God does that with wild flowers, won't God also take
equally decent care of you, as well as your wardrobe?

As for job security and college tuition and retirement
funds, those are all tomorrow's anxieties. Don't be anxious today about tomorrow; God will take care of you. Just
remember, God's way of taking care of you is one day at
a time. So don't worry!

This command, "Do not worry about your life," is not an
invitation to dump your prescription pills, forgo all financial
planning, and waltz into classrooms or interview offices
unprepared. Jesus is speaking to something deeper. Our anxieties are always matters of the heart. They reflect the fear that
there is something out there, or someone out there, waiting to
pounce upon us and destroy us. Anxiety is a matter of the
heart, for it raises the question of trust. Whom do we trust?
In the end, do we bet our lives on ourselves or on God?

We live in the world; it's our home. Christians see the universe as God's place. Each of us writes a story, an autobiog-
raphy, a personal history. Yet much of what we write is the
tale of our response to outside forces and circumstances
affecting us from beyond our making. History is God's project! Jesus says, "Do not worry about your life." You are
God's child. You live in God's world. Live as if this world
were a safe place.

The key to living as if this world were a safe place is to live
with your hand in God's hand. Jesus put it this way: "Where

your treasure is, there you heart will be also" (Matt. 6:21). If we treasure things, we will reap anxiety. The antidote to anxiety is to allow Jesus Christ to take our hand and put it back into the hand of our heavenly Father.

Amazing things happen when we put our hand into the hand of Jesus Christ and dare to live as if this world were a safe place. We find ourselves no longer alone and on our own. We feel free! Free of worry, free to take risks and embrace daring adventures; free to dream!

Listen again to Jesus: "Look at the birds of the air. . . . Consider the lilies of the field." In my mind, I see Jesus sitting on a hillside beside the Sea of Galilee. As he looks out over that pristine landscape, with the waters of a lake dancing in the distance, he notices wildflowers swaying in the breeze as singing birds make music for his ears. Suddenly Jesus begins to imagine life as God dreamed it to be: free of worry and anxiety. My hunch is that sitting behind these words is a daydreaming Jesus.

When we begin to live as if this world were a safe place, something happens to us. We begin to dream, to daydream! We imagine things not as they are but as they might be! We catch the connection between things visible and things invisible. We discover the holy in the mundane and the ordinary! We discover the kingdom in the present amidst the birdfeeder in the backyard, the wildflowers in the woods, the conversation with the friend at the mailbox or a high school locker, sitting around a dinner table with family or friends, reading a story to children or grandchildren.

The writer Frederick Buechner calls dreaming and daydreaming, his "Magic Kingdom." He says that "what is magic about it . . . is that if you look at it through the right pair of eyes it points to a kingdom more magic still," namely, to God's kingdom![5]

Buechner tells this story. He was driving to Pennsylvania for a speaking engagement. It was a lovely summer day, with the foliage greener than ever before, the sun shining through the trees, and the air waving the leafy branches like giant plumes saying, "Hello! Hello! Hello!" For just a moment, Buechner was so caught up in the ecstasy of the moment that he took a hand off the steering wheel and waved back, "Hello! Hello! Hello!" He writes:

> I was not just being eccentric. I believe that for a little while I saw those trees as so real that I was myself made real by them. We were concentric. It was the whole of me that waved at the whole of them. Trees and humans together, we have both proceeded from the hand of Holiness.[6]

We were created, you and I, to live life whole. In a world temporarily broken, it is daydreaming that frees us to imagine life as God intends life to be!

As I sat pondering this text, a series of names and faces began to parade across my mind. They were people who have emotional and spiritual intelligence. They were also people who carry scars. They have known the wounds of disappointment, having lived through the pains of untimely deaths and unfair defeats. Yet they live life with verve, as if this world were a safe place. Why? Because in their worst moments they discovered that no one and no place is safe from God's grace and loving presence.

In his novel *Mariette in Ecstasy,* Ron Hansen tells the story of a seventeen-year-old, Mariette Baptiste, who is a postulant in the convent of the Sisters of the Crucifixion. The convent is a safe place, mysterious and strange, but safe from a menacing world. In this little fort, the nuns go about their business. Outside sits a dangerous world with its ominous presence. One day, the presence invades the convent. As Mariette scrubs the floor, blood begins to drip from holes in her hands. She bandages the wounds, but they continue to seep. In time, she seeks out the priest for counsel. "Look at what Jesus is doing to me!" she exclaims.

Instantly, the convent is in turmoil. No one knows what to do with this young postulant and her supposed stigmata of the crucified Christ. Most of the sisters grow jealous. The mother superior, convinced that Mariette is simply being self-serving, expels her from the convent. The wounds then disappear as mysteriously as they appeared. Distraught and brokenhearted, Mariette picks up the pieces of her life as she makes her way back into the world beyond the convent. She keeps house for her father, tends the garden, fixes dinner, minds the cat, plays canasta, goes grocery shopping. Thirty years pass. One of the young novices who had befriended Mariette becomes the prioress of the convent. Mariette writes Mother Philomene a letter congratulating her, recalling some of the good times they had shared together. Mariette then concludes her letter with these words: "Christ still sends me roses. We try to be formed and held and kept by him; but instead he offers us freedom. Now, when I try to know his will, his kindness floods me, his great love overwhelms me, and I hear him whisper, 'Surprise me! Surprise me! Surprise me!'"[7]

Chapter 10

Living as if You Were
a Really Good Person

*Unless your righteousness exceeds that of the scribes
and Pharisees, you will never enter the kingdom of heaven.*

—Matt. 5:20

*J*ust over twenty years ago, I began my ministry at Second Presbyterian Church in Indianapolis. I will never forget the day. It was Wednesday, April 1, 1981; April Fools Day; about four o'clock in the afternoon. I had driven alone from Chicago, where my family was remaining to finish out the school year. I was to stay in the home of a family who was wintering in Florida. I drove my car, spilling over with books and clothes, down the drive to the garage in the back of the house. I parked the car, and walked up the drive toward the front door when I noticed four people walking toward me. How nice, a welcoming committee, I thought. As they came closer it became clear that theirs was no welcoming mission. These must be four of the people who voted against me, I speculated. I'd been warned that a candid, unvarnished conscience was as much a Hoosier characteristic as was friendliness and hospitality. There I stood, surrounded by four icy strangers. "Who are you?" one of them demanded. "I'm Bill Enright," I replied as I held out a hand, which they ignored. "What are you doing here?" barked another. I explained that

I was the new pastor of Second Presbyterian Church, the church with the spire you could see just through the woods and over the creek. "You sure about that?" snapped the third. "Not as certain as I was five minutes ago," I said. Relaxing, the strangers then informed me that there had been an armed robbery at the end of the street the previous weekend, with two people tied up in their home as it was burglarized.

Later, as I watched the four vigilantes disappear into their homes, I said to myself, "Bill Enright, if you are to survive in Indianapolis you're going to have to be on your best behavior. You're going to have to work at being a really good person because these Hoosiers appear to have difficulty distinguishing robbers from preachers."

What does it mean to be a Christian? Of course, Christians are disciples of Jesus Christ, people who have bet their lives on this God who has come to us in Christ. I would hope that the street answer to that question would also have something to do with being good. Christians are people who try to live as if they were *really good people*.

Apparently, the congregation of Christians to whom Matthew first wrote was uncertain what it meant to live as a disciple of Jesus Christ. So Matthew collected into one piece, called the Sermon on the Mount, many of Jesus' teachings about what it means to be a church, to be a disciple of Jesus Christ. In a nutshell, what Jesus said was this: Disciples are people who live as if they were living in the kingdom of God right now. They live as if God were at their fingertips. They live as if heaven were theirs to make here on earth. They live as if everyone around them was also part of God's kingdom. They have a daring sense of adventure about them, so they live as if this world were a safe place. In short, disciples try to live as if they were really good people. Jesus put it this way: "Unless your righteousness exceeds that of the scribes and Pharisees, you will never enter the kingdom of heaven."

"Righteousness," or *dikaiosune*, is the same word Plato uses in his *Republic* to describe the good life and the really good person. So when Jesus says, "Unless your righteousness exceeds that of the scribes and the Pharisees," he is describing disciples as people who live with their lives intentionally tilted toward goodness.[1]

Deep in most of us simmers the desire to be a good person. But good and bad short-circuit each other in the wiring of our beings. The ethicist and theologian Lewis Smedes tells the story of his brother's dying of a brain tumor. After being diagnosed, he had approximately one year to live. Smedes asked him what he was going to do with himself. The brother replied, "I'm thinking about something; but I . . . feel a little silly talking about it. . . . What I want is to become a better person than I've been." Smedes writes, "It wasn't at all what I expected him to say . . . or what I wanted him to say. I wanted him to talk about sailing . . . about seeing sunsets . . . visiting Ireland . . . touching people . . . hearing music, seeing the scenery . . . I wanted him to forget about being good."[2] But we can't forget. We can't forget goodness, for we humans are people who have been created in the image of God. That means that we have been created in the image of goodness itself. So disciples of Jesus try to live as if we were good people.

What does it mean to try to live as if we were really good? Let's examine Matthew 5:20–48 through three different pairs of glasses. First, read what Jesus says in terms of the ordinary people of his day. For them, the law and the keeping of the law was the measuring stick for the good life. Jesus says that if we want to be just good enough to stay out of trouble then all we have to do is live by the rules. Don't murder (v. 21), don't commit adultery (v. 27), make certain your divorce is proper and legal (v. 31), and keep the promises you make in God's name (v. 33). When you are attacked, retaliate, but only in kind; only do to other persons what they have done to you (v. 38). Hate your enemy, but love your neighbor (v. 43).

A second way to read Matthew 5:20–48 is as a disciple of Jesus. Jesus wants his followers to be a cut above the norm; he wants them to live as if they were really good people. He says don't lose your temper (v. 22), don't sexually fantasize about other people (v. 28), don't divorce (v. 32), keep all the promises you make, even those oaths you did not make in God's name (v. 34), don't retaliate or even try to get even (v. 39), and love your enemies (v. 44).

The third way to read this passage is through the lens of our world. When I do that, I am absolutely mesmerized by how "right on" Jesus is when it comes to our struggle to be good. The subjects talked about are uncanny in their time-lessness and universality. Jesus is talking about the headlines of our world today: violence (vv. 21–26), pornography and sexual misconduct (vv. 27–30), domestic abandonment and marital chaos (vv. 31-32), the want of integrity and honesty in our culture (vv. 33–37), the conundrum we call victimization (vv. 38–42), and the tragedy of racial prejudice and ethnic cleansings (vv. 43–48).

As I reflect on what Jesus is saying, I find six questions staring me in my face as I struggle to be a good person:

1. How do I handle my anger in ways that are appropriate and not disruptive?
2. How do I live with my sexual desires in ways that are wholesome and not seductive?
3. How do I resolve my marital spats in ways that are redemptive and caring?
4. How good is my word? How do I keep the promises I make?
5. How do I respond to personal and injurious attacks so as not to escalate the incident?
6. What does it mean for me to love my enemies, those people I don't like?

Disciples live with these questions. These are the questions that keep us honest in our pursuit of goodness.

The Canadian theologian Douglas John Hall reminds us that the image of God is not so much a noun as it is a verb. It is not so much something we are as it is something we do or fail to do. It is not a set of qualities bequeathed to us as humans; it is a relationship to our Creator to be mirrored in our everyday living. We were made to mirror God's goodness in our world.[3] How do we do that? We image God! We imagine! We practice! We pray!

Image! A university chaplain was having dinner with some students and found himself sitting next to a very large football player. The young man told him he was studying sports theory. "What's sports theory?" the chaplain inquired. The young man said that it had something to do with imaging, with getting the brain to play through all the right plays again and again, so that, come the game, his responses would be automatic. The imagination, he said, has everything to do with how you perform.

Sitting across the table was a piano player who said she did the same thing. She told how she practices without actually being at the piano. She simply images the piano in her head as she sits down and allows her fingers to do the walking and dancing along the imaginary keyboard.[4]

When you get up in the morning, image your day. Walk through your schedule and imagine yourself handling each moment with poise and grace. Whether at home or work or school or on holiday, allow all the possible scenarios of your day to play in your mind as you shower or drive. In each instance, ask yourself how goodness itself might respond, and imagine yourself responding that way.

Practice! As my friend Craig Dykstra reminds us, the Christian faith is physical. It is a body of faith that involves "gestures, moves, going certain places and doing certain things." Just as you learn basketball by playing basketball, so you learn goodness in living by doing it, by chasing moral excellence.[5]

Anthony Parks is a dot-com multimillionaire. He never went to college. Most of his life he worked as a waiter until a venture capital Internet company, Webvan, hired him to head customer service. Last year, Webvan went public, and the rest is history. Unlike many of his Silicon Valley peers, however, Anthony Parks did not spend his money on himself. He began to give it away. To date, he has given away shares of Webvan stock to more than seventy-five people; his gifts ranging from one hundred to five thousand shares each. Recently Parks went to New York to talk to kids in the Bronx about the value of a decent education. With him was Charlie Ward of the New York Knicks. While Parks was waiting for Ward to sign autographs, a boy on crutches came up to him and asked for his autograph. Parks was overwhelmed, saying, "Nobody, and I mean nobody, has ever asked for my autograph." He obliged the boy. Upon learning that the lad suffered from a debilitating bone disease, Parks was heard to say, "I've got to figure out something special I can do for him."[6] Goodness is something you practice at, and the more you practice, the more natural it becomes.

Practice, however, does not make perfect. The Bible reminds us that no one is righteous. None of us is perfect when it comes to being good. Christians practice being good not to master life but to mirror God's presence within themselves and in their world. None of us will ever get beyond the need of grace and divine forgiveness. But, all things considered, practice can leave us better than we would otherwise be.

Pray! Prayer is what picks us up when we have messed up. Prayer is how God's presence and Spirit ooze into our souls to reshape our anxieties. Prayer opens us to a presence and a power from beyond ourselves. Prayer takes the pressure off of us to do good on our own. Prayer puts God and life, goodness and grace, the tension between wanting to do good and actually doing it, into perspective.

In my twenty years in Indianapolis, I've been blessed to know some really good people. Gerda was one of those people. This winter I celebrated her funeral. For the occasion I read "A Mother Superior's Prayer," which she kept taped to her mirror:

> Lord, Thou knowest better than I know myself that
> I am growing older and will some day be old.
> Keep me from getting talkative, and particularly from
> the fatal habit of thinking I must say something
> on every subject and on every occasion.
> Release me from craving to try to straighten out
> everybody's affairs.
> Make me thoughtful, but not moody; helpful,
> but not bossy. . . .
> Keep me reasonably sweet; I do not want to be a
> saint—some of them are so hard to live with,
> but a sour old woman is one of the crowning
> works of the devil.
> Help me to extract all possible fun out of life. There
> are so many funny things around us, and I don't
> want to miss any of them. Amen.

In her novel *Saint Maybe,* Anne Tyler tells the story of a young man named Ian Bedloe. Ian feels responsible for the deaths of his brother and sister-in-law, who have left behind two children. In his guilt, Ian meets with an eccentric preacher, Reverend Emmett. Ian confesses what has happened, after which he says, "Don't you think I'm forgiven?" "Goodness, no," Reverend Emmett replies. "You can't just say, 'I'm sorry, God.' Why anyone could do that much! You have to offer reparation—concrete, practical reparation. Jesus helps us undo what can't be undone only after we have done what we can to make amends. . . . See to those children."

While that is about the most un-Presbyterian thing Ian, a Presbyterian, has ever heard, he does it. He drops out of college and takes on fathering a bunch of kids. He fixes their meals, watches them grow up, helps them through their various crises, finds satisfaction in caring for them. By the end of the novel, Daphne, the difficult older daughter who had been adopted, says of Ian, "I think he's a saint . . . maybe!"[7]

"Unless your righteousness exceeds that of the scribes and the Pharisees, you will never enter the kingdom of heaven." In this Sermon on the Mount, Jesus is taking ordinary people like you and me and making of us something more than we would otherwise be. Jesus wants to turn us into really good people. Maybe even saints!

Chapter 11

Living as if God
Were Your Only Audience

*Beware of practicing your piety before others
in order to be seen by them. . . . Your Father
who sees in secret will reward you.*

—Matt. 6:1, 4

t happens to me now and again on the golf course, as in times past it happened on the tennis court or the basketball floor. A person I'm playing with loses and goes into a tirade, unleashing a string of swear words. Then he looks at me and remembers that I'm a minister. As embarrassment flushes his face, he mutters, "Geez, Rev, sorry about that; I just forgot that you're a preacher." For just a moment, I feel like some sort of alien. Then, laughing, I usually say, "Oh, forget it. Besides, there's nothing wrong with having a conversation with the Almighty, even on a golf course." One day, following such a moment of divine elocution, a person made a comment that still puzzles me: "It's all right, pastor. I cuss a little and you pray a little, but neither one of us means anything by it."

Too frequently, we who call ourselves Christians don't mean anything by it. For Jesus, however, belief in God means something. As Jesus sees it, disciples are people who live with a difference because they allow their imaginations to shape their living. They imagine themselves to be living in the kingdom of God now, so they live as if heaven were here on earth. They imagine this world to be a safe place, so they chase life with a mix of daring and compassion. They imagine themselves as really good people, because living as a Christian means something to them. The key to their living life with such godly imagination is this: They never forget their audience. They live as if God were their only audience. Jesus put it this way: "Beware of practicing your piety before others in order to be seen by them. . . . Your Father who sees in secret will reward you."

In Matthew 6:1–6, Jesus talks about two practices common to most people: the giving of money, or philanthropy, and the reality of prayer, or piety. As Jesus sees it, disciples pursue these practices—but with a difference.

Jesus assumes that giving money away is part of the practice of living as both a Christian and a responsible citizen. Note how the text reads: not *if,* but *when* you give alms. In the world of Jesus' day, people were expected to give to charity. Disciples give away money, but with a unique spirit. They don't give away money to make a public name for themselves as if they could buy respectability.

Recently I received my tax documents from my accountant. As I went over my tax return, I made an amazing discovery. I found Matthew 6:2 plumb in the middle of my long form, Schedule A, lines 15 through 18. The Greek word translated "to give alms" is the same as our English word *eleemosynary,* which means "charitable giving," or as Schedule A words it, "gifts for charity."

Disciples of Jesus Christ give generously, but not for tax purposes. Disciples of Jesus Christ give away all the money they can in order to make the presence of God's kingdom a reality in the world beyond their front door. Disciples write big checks because the account from which they draw is the ocean of God's generosity.

Disciples also pray! They don't just think about prayer;

they pray. They pray to open the house of their souls to the presence of God. They don't pray to impress others with their piety. They pray to make God's kingdom a reality within themselves and the world that occupies their concerns and interests. They pray, not to make a religious name for themselves, but to bend God's ear to their world. It is prayer that detaches us from the distracting world of dollars and the demands of to-do lists and puts perspective on our wants and wishes.

Why is it important for us as Christians to give away our money and practice our prayers with a difference? Because most people are not good at giving money and praying. We are stingy when it comes to charitable giving. We have lived through the longest bull run in the history of the stock market. Ironically, amidst this great economic boom, the national percentage of income given to charity has declined. When it comes to prayer, most people are too busy or preoccupied to make the practice of prayer part of their life. As Bill Gates recently put it, "In terms of allocation of time resources, religion is not very efficient. There's a lot more I could be doing on Sunday morning."

Jesus makes a stunning observation concerning the practices of giving away money and praying. When it comes to the practice of philanthropy and piety, many people get caught up in the respectability trap. They use their charitable contributions to try to gain public respectability. They pray and parade their piety in public in an attempt to gain religious respectability. The upshot is, their actions backfire on them. Their sincerity is questioned.

With tongue in cheek, Jesus pokes fun at such people. Humorously, he describes one person as blowing a trumpet as he or she parades through the streets toward the church, charitable contribution waving in hand. With equal wit, he portrays a dowdy sourpuss holding a street corner pray-in to impress the community with his or her piety. Jesus says,

"Beware of practicing your piety before others in order to be seen by them."

But people do. We pay to have our names pasted to public buildings. In my town of Indianapolis I think of the RCA Dome, the Hilbert Theatre, the Conseco Fieldhouse. Amidst great hoopla, Bill Gates, severely criticized for his tight-fistedness as the richest man in the world, set up his own foundation. With equal fanfare, Ted Turner gave an estimated one billion dollars to the United Nations. Both leave the impression that their gifts are driven more by public relations savvy than honest-to-God charitable convictions. When the line between advertising and philanthropy blurs, civic pride and corporate integrity both suffer. The most authentically generous people I have known give quietly and often anonymously.

A news story recently caught my eye and set this text free to dance in my mind. For sixty-two years, Herman Wells was the president and chancellor of Indiana University but had just died. It was announced that in 2005 the main library in Bloomington will be renamed after him. Why the five-year wait? Because of the respectability trap. It was a Herman Wells dictum that no building or site be named for a person until five years after that person's death. I think Herman Wells, who was a master at fund-raising, understood well these words of Jesus: "Beware of practicing your piety before others in order to be seen by them."

But most people do. We religious folk are particularly adept at parading our piety to gain public religious respect. We hold pray-ins and make pious public pronouncements, I fear, more often to play politics rather than to seek God's wisdom. We too easily identify God's cause with our cause, misrepresenting our will as God's will. Sometimes we deliberately sprinkle our speech with religious phrases to con other people into doing business with us or, if we are politicians, into voting for us.

We preachers are particularly vulnerable to the respectability trap. We rightly sense that the currency that counts in God's kingdom is more spiritual than monetary. Sadly, we confuse sanctimoniousness with spirituality. On Sundays, we don our pompous robes and pious masks and change into unctuous voices to look and act and sound like God Almighty. In so doing, we focus the spotlight on ourselves rather than God. We forget our audience of one!

Jesus uses a unique word to describe this respectability trap: *hypocrite*. In Matthew, Jesus is quoted as using the word fifteen times. The word *hypocrite* originated with the theater and was used to describe an actor, someone playing a role. However, Jesus is not talking about the theater. Jesus is talking about people who are so caught up with themselves that they take themselves much too seriously. A better way to translate this word *hypocrite* is "overly scrupulous." Overly scrupulous people are punctilious and pompous to a fault.[1] They are so intent on things being done their way, which they call the right way, that they set themselves up as models of righteousness and propriety. C. S. Lewis describes such overly scrupulous people as folk who live life with a "total absence of charity and trust." They live caught in the respectability trap.[2]

In her short story "Revelation," Flannery O'Connor tells the story of one such overly scrupulous person. Ruby Turpin was a respectable, hard-working, church-going woman with an uppity sense of her own righteousness. She was one of those people who "when she couldn't sleep occupied herself with the question of who she would have chosen to be if she couldn't have been herself." As Ruby looked at life, there were three kinds of people: white trash, poor blacks, and folks like herself with "manners, her pleasant disposition and her positive outlook toward life."[3]

Ruby is sitting in the doctor's waiting room with her taciturn husband, Claud. A radio is playing soft gospel music as Ruby begins to size up the people sitting in the small waiting room. There is a stylish well-dressed gray-haired lady with her fat and pimply daughter of eighteen, maybe nineteen, who sits scowling behind a book. Most are "white-trashy folk." A "red-headed youngish woman" vigorously works a piece of chewing gum. A thin, leathery old woman in a cotton-print dress and tennis shoes sits. A lean, stringy old fellow appears to be half-asleep. A lank-faced, gritty-looking woman in a yellow sweatshirt and wine-colored slacks, with her dirty yellow hair tied with a piece of red paper ribbon, sits next to her child who is slumped in his seat, his nose running unchecked. You can guess the one person with whom Ruby carries on a conversation—the stylish woman with the scowling daughter. Ruby is also intent on engaging the woman's daughter in conversation. Ruby learns that the girl's name is Mary Grace. The mother tells her that the girl goes to college up north in Massachusetts, a place called Wellesley. As Ruby chatters on, she makes comments about everything and everyone, putting the people in the room into their proper place in her pecking order of life. Turning again to the girl, Ruby says, "It never hurt anyone to smile. . . . If it's one thing I am, it's grateful. When I think of all I could have been besides myself, . . . I just feel like shouting, 'Thank you, Jesus, for making everything the way it is!' "[4]

That is when the book hits Ruby between the eyes, sending her sprawling on the floor. The next thing Ruby remembers is the girl whispering in her ear, "Go back to hell where you came from, you old warthog." That night, as Ruby lays in bed with a damp washcloth over her eyes, she keeps repeating to herself, "I am not a warthog from hell. I am not a warthog from hell."[5]

The next day Ruby staggers to the hog pen, or the "pig parlor" as she proudly calls it. As she stares at the pigs in their pen she asks, "How am I a hog and me both? How am I saved and from hell, too?" As she stands there, she has a vision of heaven. She takes note of the procession. Souls rumbling toward heaven. Companies of white trash, clean for the first time. Bands of black folk in white robes. Battalions of lunatics leaping like frogs. And bringing up the rear, a tribe of people like herself and Claud. Suddenly Ruby sees herself as she is, "saved . . . but a warthog from hell" who has missed out on the joy of the Christian life because of the respectability trap.[6]

When we forget the audience of one to whom we are to play our lives, we too get caught in the respectability trap. When we remember that our audience of one consists of the God who sees everything in secret, we are free to live, free to be ourselves, and, yes, free to give away money as we should and pray as we ought without any need for fanfare or self-serving public commercials.

Gerret Keizer tells the true story of a woman who lived in the remote town of Victory, Vermont, a town without a church, a store, or a school. Its claim to fame was twofold: its sizable bog and its status as the last town in Vermont to receive electricity. During the course of earning her master's degree, the woman had to commute several times a week to the state university in Burlington, a good hundred miles away. Each night as she came home she would see an old man sitting by the side of her road. He was always there no matter how horrid the weather. He never acknowledged the passing of her car; he just sat there like a gnarled old tree, his cap and shoulders covered with snow.

Curious about who this man was and what brought him to the same spot each evening, she inquired of a neighbor, "Have you ever seen an old man who sits by the road late at night?" "Oh, yes, many times," replied her neighbor. "Is he . . . a little touched upstairs? Does he ever go home?" Laughing, the neighbor replied, "He's no more touched than you or I. And he goes home right after you do. You see, he doesn't like the idea of your driving by yourself out late all alone on these back roads; so, every night he walks out to wait for you. When he sees your tail-light disappear around the bend, and he knows you're OK, he goes home to bed."[7]

My hunch is that the more adept we become at playing our lives to God, the more invisible we also become.

Notes

CHAPTER 1

1. Douglas Ottati, "Millennial Reflections on an Interdependent World," *The Christian Century*, 22 December 1999, 1254f.

2. Bharati Mukherijee, "Words," *New York Times Magazine*, 5 December 1999, 182.

3. *The Study Catechism* (Louisville, Ky.: Geneva Press, 1998), question 94.

4. Jostein Gaarder, *The Solitaire Mystery* (New York: Berkley Books, 1996), 178.

5. John Calvin, *Institutes of the Christian Religion* (Philadelphia: Westminster Press, 1960), 2.8.1ff.

6. Walter Brueggemann, *Theology of the Old Testament* (Minneapolis: Fortress, 1997), 572, 574.

7. Stanley Hauerwas and William Willimon, *The Truth About God* (Nashville: Abingdon Press, 1999), 19–20.

8. John Donne, "Hymn to God the Father," in *The Norton Anthology of English Literature,* 4th ed., vol. 1, ed. M. H. Abrams et al. (New York: W. W. Norton & Co., 1979), 1104.

CHAPTER 2

1. *The Study Catechism*, question 98.

2. Sally Quinn, "The G-Word and the A List," section C, p. 2, *Washington Post*, 12 July 1999.

3. "The Jesus Card," *Christian Century*, 5 January 2000, 5.

4. Quoted in Robert Coles, *The Secular Mind* (Princeton, N.J.: Princeton University Press, 1999), 102.

5. *Ibid.*, 162, 164–165.

6. David Herbert Donald, *Lincoln* (New York: Simon & Schuster, 1995), 354, 376.

7. Quoted in *Context,* a bimonthly publication of quotes and observations by Martin E. Marty on Religion and Culture, 1 February 1999.

CHAPTER 3

1. Eugene Peterson, *Working the Angles,* (Grand Rapids: Wm. B. Eerdmans Publishing Co., 1987), 67.

2. Jon Winokur, *The Portable Curmudgeon* (New York: New American Library, 1987), 271.

3. Dorothy Bass, *Receiving the Day* (San Francisco: Jossey-Bass, 2000), 11.

4. Karl Barth, *Church Dogmatics* (Edinburgh: T. & T. Clark, 1960), 3.4.53.

5. Bass, *Receiving the Day,* 83–84.

6. Samuel Balentine, *The Torah's Vision of Worship* (Minneapolis: Fortress Press, 1999), 243. Chapter 9 of this book, p. 235ff is an excellent essay on worship and Sabbath.

7. Dorothy Bass, *Practicing Our Faith: A Way of Life for a Searching People* (San Francisco: Jossey-Bass, 1997), 80–81.

8. Tilden Edwards, *Sabbath Time* (New York: Seabury Press, 1982), 20.

CHAPTER 4

1. Oliver Sacks, *The Man Who Mistook His Wife for a Hat* (New York: HarperCollins, 1990), 23, 29.

2. Shirley Abbott, *Womenfolks: Growing Up Down South* (Boston: Houghton Mifflin, 1998), 9.

3. Sacks, *Man Who Mistook His Wife,* 29.

4. Jean Illsley Clarke, *Self-Esteem: A Family Affair* (Minneapolis: Winston Press) 1.

5. David Popenoe, quoted in K. Brynolf Lyon and Archie Smith Jr., *Tending the Flock* (Louisville, Ky.: Westminster John Knox Press, 1998), 1.

6. Heather McDonald, *An Almost Holy Picture.* From the original manuscript, performed at Indianapolis Repertory Theatre, January 2000.

CHAPTER 5

1. P. D. James, *The Children of Men* (New York: Alfred A. Knopf, 1993), 3–6

2. *The Virus of Violence,* Nineteenth Star LLC 2000.

3. Quoted in Charles Colson, "Why Fidelity Matters," *Christianity Today,* 27 April 1998, 104.

4. Annie Dillard, *For The Time Being* (New York: Alfred A. Knopf, 1999), 200.

5. *Study Catechism*, question 108.

6. Quoted in Hauerwas and Willimon, *Truth about God,* 91.

7. Ibid.

8. *Monday Morning,* 7 November 1983.

9. Timothy C. Morgan, "Have We Become Too Busy with Death?" *Christianity Today,* 7 February 2000, 39.

10. Kevin Galvin, "Clinton Bans Genetic Test Bias," *Indianapolis Star,* 9 February 2000, A3.

11. Hauerwas and Willimon, *Truth about God,* 103.

12. John Polkinghorne, *Serious Talk: Science and Religion in Dialogue* (Harrisburg, Pa.: Trinity Press International, 1995), 75.

13. I am indebted to Dr. Robert Payton, dean emeritus of the Indiana University School of Philanthropy, for this reference.

14. *Virus of Violence.*

15. James, *Children of Men,* 155

16. Ibid., p. 241.

CHAPTER 6

1. Saul Bellow, *Henderson the Rain King* (New York: Penguin Books, 1996), 81.

2. Ibid., 24.

3. Calvin, *Institutes*, 2.8.45.

4. *Study Catechism,* question 114.

5. Hauerwas and Willimon, *Truth about God,* 134.

6. Stephen L. Carter, *Civility* (New York: Basic Books, 1998), 277ff.

7. Calvin, *Institutes,* 2.8.46.

8. *Study Catechism,* question 117.

9. *New Encyclopaedia Britannica,* 15th ed., 904–6.

10. Adam Smith, *The Theory of Moral Sentiments* (Indianapolis: Liberty Classics, 1982), 15–17.

11. Bellow, *Henderson the Rain King,* 381.

CHAPTER 7

1. Herman Melville, *Moby Dick* (New York: Literary Guild of America, 1949), 1–4.

2. For a graphic telling of this story from Luke 5, see Walter Wangerin, *The Book of God* (Grand Rapids: Zondervan Publishing House, 1996), 642–43.

3. C. S. Lewis, "Theology," in *The Joyful Christian* (New York: Simon & Schuster, 1977), 34.

4. For an incisive treatment of the Great Commandment see Patrick Miller, *Deuteronomy* (Louisville, Ky.: John Knox Press, 1990), 97–98.

5. C. S. Lewis, "Love Thy Neighbor," in *Joyful Christian,* 197.

6. Philip Yancey, "Why I Don't Go to a Megachurch," *Christianity Today*, 20 May 1996, 80.

7. Ibid.

8. Carter, *Civility,* 62–63.

CHAPTER 8

1. Dallas Willard, *The Divine Conspiracy* (New York: Harper-Collins, 1998), 36.

2. C. S. Lewis, *Mere Christianity* (New York: Macmillan, 1956), 147

3. Ibid., 174.

4. Calvin, *Institutes*, 3.3.9, 3.20.42.

5. Michael Murphy, *Golf in the Kingdom* (New York: Dell Publishing, 1972), 12–33.

6. Philip Yancey, *The Jesus I Never Knew* (Grand Rapids: Zondervan Publishing House, 1995), 130.

7. Ibid., 144.

CHAPTER 9

1. Daniel Goleman, "What Makes a Leader," *Harvard Business Review,* November–December 1998, 93ff.

2. Mark Shepard, "Leaders with a High 'EQ' Rise to the Top, in Part Because They Understand People," *Life @ Work*, March/April 2000, 66–67.

3. Peter J. Gomes, *The Good Book* (New York: William Morrow & Company, 1996), 179.

4. Thomas G. Long, *Matthew* (Louisville, Ky.: Westminster John Knox Press, 1997), 74.

5. Frederick Buechner, *The Eyes of the Heart* (San Francisco: HarperSanFrancisco, 1999), 183.

6. Frederick Buechner, *The Longing for Home* (New York: HarperCollins, 1996), 112–13.

7. Ron Hansen, *Mariette In Ecstasy* (New York: HarperPerennial, 1992), 179.

CHAPTER 10

1. Willard, *Divine Conspiracy*, 145.

2. Lewis B. Smedes, *A Pretty Good Person* (New York: Harper & Row, 1990), 173–74.

3. Douglas John Hall, *Professing the Faith* (Minneapolis: Fortress, 1993), 216

4. Gomes, *Good Book*, 200.

5. Craig Dykstra, *Growing in the Life of Faith* (Louisville, Ky.: Geneva Press, 1999), 71.

6. George Anders, "A Dot-Com Millionaire Shares His Jackpot," *Wall Street Journal*, 7 April 2000, B1, B4.

7. Anne Tyler, *Saint Maybe* (New York: Alfred A. Knopf, 1991), 122–23.

CHAPTER 11

1. W. F. Albright and C. S. Mann, *Matthew* (Garden City, N.Y.: Doubleday & Co., 1971), cxxi, 73.

2. C. S. Lewis, "Scruples," in *Joyful Christian*, 80.

3. Flannery O'Connor, "Revelation" in *Every Thing That Rises Must Converge* (New York: Noonday Press, 1965), 195.

4. Ibid., 205 6.

5. Ibid., 207.

6. Ibid., 215.

7. Gerret Keizer, "Watchers in the Night" *Christian Century*, 5 April 2000, 381.